# THE MYTH

*of*

# PAPAL INFALLIBILITY

"Can you show me in this great City of Rome anyone who would receive you as pope if they had not received gold or silver for it?"
— St. Bernard

"The entire world knows how profitable this fable of Christ has been to us and ours."
— Pope Leo X (1513-1521)

ISBN 0-912927-41-0

Exclusive Distributor and Printer:
**The St. John of Kronstadt Press**
Rt. 1 Box 205
Liberty, TN 37095

Printed in
The United States of America

Some will read the following essay and express doubts as to the authenticity of the quotes, sources, or the materials presented for review. To them we can only state unequivocally — after nine years of research — that:

The documentation presented on these few pages is taken from factual accounts. The statements — from historical sources — are quoted without alteration or omission.

Nothing has been fabricated to advance our particular views. All material has been laid out before you honestly and with humble hope that, in the final analysis, truth will prevail.

— The Author

"If we also say, Thou art the Christ, the Son of the Living God, then we also become Peter... for whoever assimilates to Christ, becomes the Rock. Does Christ give the keys of the Kingdom to Peter alone, whereas other blessed people cannot receive them?"

— Origen, Homily on Matthew: XII, X

(Origen was the most respected teacher of the Greek Fathers on Biblical commentary. He lived c. 185-254.)

"The Church exists in history because man believes in Christ, the Son of God. Without this faith, there can be no Church. Peter was the first to confess this faith, and thus became the 'first Christian'... to the extent, however, that this title depends on a man's faith, a man can also lose it. This is what happened to Peter, and he had to undergo tears of repentance before he was re-established in his dignity."

— John Meyendorff, The Primacy of Peter, p. 14

"The pope is Christ in office, Christ in jurisdiction and power... We bow down before thy voice, O Holy Father, as we would before Christ Himself...the voice of Christ, the God of truth; in clinging to thee, we cling to Christ."

— Jan. 9, 1870, Vatican I Official Proclamation

This is a sourcebook — a collection of Scriptural quotations, historical statements, summaries of thought, and explanations of fact.

It is not written as a monograph or novel. It is loosely structured so as to give readers access to historical materials while allowing them the opportunity to extract quotes and commentary without doing violence to the original material or its context.

It has several features of note:

(1) its major theme is infallibility and the supposed universal jurisdiction of the Bishop of Rome.

(2) it contains a number of Scriptural translations, since the author did not wish to take anything from the original texts or transcribe items simply to suit a premise.

(3) it is repetitive in parts because this short thesis — maintaining that infallibility is a myth — is told and re-told and excised in various ways. This type of construction was utilized to reinforce our sincere contention that the dogma of infallibility and universal jurisdiction is TOTALLY FALSE AND SPURIOUS. What may seem to be repetition is actually *emphasis*.

Throughout this work the terms primacy, primacy of jurisdiction and infallibility are used many times. However, there are certain distinctions to be made:

*primacy* can refer either to "primacy of honor", which grants to Rome the simple recognition that her bishop had jurisdiction in the chief city of the Empire, a "primus inter pares" (first among *equals*), or to

*primacy of jurisdiction*, which refers to the supposed right of the Bishop of Rome to speak and act legislatively for *all* Christians in *all* Churches.

*Infallibility* means the right, divinely given, of the Roman Pontiffs to interpret the faith and define the truth "of themselves, and not by virtue of the consent of the Church (and these definitions are) irreformable." This is the claim of the papacy.

Since nothing in quotes or direct translations has been changed, and since some authors assume that the reader understands the subtle differences in terms, the reader must look to the context of the quote and make the necessary translations.

In the late nineteenth century, Ignaz von Döllinger of Germany was recognized throughout the world as the greatest Church historian of his day, bar none.  So as not to compromise his integrity, Dr. Döllinger left the Roman Catholic Church after the definition of papal infallibility in 1870.  He knew this doctrine to be an invention, historically untenable, a falsehood and a pretext to power.  Dr. von Döllinger strongly underscored that a grievous lie had been forced upon the people and now greater falsehoods must be repeated over and over to defend a horrid error.  He simply, yet as a voice crying in the wilderness, spoke to history when he announced:

"As a Christian, as a theologian, as a historian, as a citizen, I cannot accept this doctrine."

To Dr. von Döllinger this feeble effort is dedicated.

---

"Beloved, when I gave all diligence to write unto you of the common salvation, it was needful for me to write unto you, and exhort you that *we should earnestly contend (debate) for the faith which was once delivered unto the saints.*"

—Epistle of Jude, 3

---

Obviously it is a good and holy thing to debate the things which dilute our faith.  Many teachings offered as "of God" are nothing but the vanities of men.  When attacked we must respond with truth, charity and vigor or what we hold to be precious becomes a beautiful vessel containing nothing of value.  In not doing so we allow priceless ointments to flow freely to the barren earth, polluted by common and crude thought.

This having been said, we offer these words for your consideration and serious thought.

---

"We teach... it is a dogma divinely revealed that the Roman pontiff... by virtue of his supreme Apostolic authority... is possessed of that infallibility which the divine Redeemer willed (for) His Church... Therefore, such definitions of the Roman Pontiff of themselves — and not by virtue of the consent of the Church — are irreformable."

—*Synopsis: Declaration of Infallibility*,
Rome, 1870. (*"Pastor æternus"*)

**"As a violent thunderstorm raged above St. Peter's Basilica in Rome on July 18, 1870, the bishops of the First Vatican Council adopted a decree that would alter Christian history... as such, the doctrine of infallibility remains a fundamental obstacle to the reunion of Christianity."**

**"Pius IX... compared opposition bishops to Pontius Pilate condemning Jesus and pleaded: 'My children, do not leave me. Cleave to me and follow me. Unite with the representative of Jesus Christ.'"**

—*Time*, 1979 (from a review of
*How the Pope Became Infallible*, by August B. Hasler)

Johann Joseph von Döllinger,
professor of Church history in Munich

# THE MYTH OF PAPAL INFALLIBILITY
## (AN HISTORICAL JOURNEY)
### A SOURCEBOOK FOR PEOPLE IN THE CHURCH

From the Gospel of St. Matthew (23:1-12):

"Then Jesus spoke to the crowds and to His disciples. The teachers of the Law and the Pharisees are the authorized interpreters of Moses' Law. So you must obey and follow everything they tell you to do. Do not, however, imitate their actions, because they do not practice what they preach. They tie onto people's backs loads that are heavy and hard to carry, yet they are not even willing to lift a finger to help them carry their loads. They do everything so that people will see them. Look at the straps with Scripture verses on them which they wear on their foreheads and arms, and notice how large they are! Notice also how long are the tassels on their cloaks! They love the best seats at feasts and the reserved places in the synagogues: they love to be greeted with respect in the market places and to have people call them 'Teacher'. You must not be called 'Teacher' because you are all brothers of one another and have only one Teacher. And you must not call anyone here on earth 'Father' *(lit: Master)* because you have only one Father in heaven. Nor should you be called 'Leader', because your one and only Leader is the Messiah. The greatest among you must be your servant. Whoever makes himself great will be humbled, and whoever humbles himself will be made great."

For twenty-nine years, during most of my adult life, I was a firm supporter and apologist for the papalist position within the Roman Catholic Church. I would defend the pope's "universal primacy" and his certain "infallibility" without question. I would argue heatedly that these things were indeed divinely-inspired and sanctioned by the Lord. I was bound up with an unrelenting devotion to the Bishop of Rome, as "Vicar of Jesus Christ" and the "Supreme Pontiff of the Universal Church".

It was only in later years that I realized there is not so much as the *simplest* historical evidence on which to base my belief in these claims and that I was arguing my position from blind faith and sheer obedience. I did not wish to admit error; therefore I supplanted anger, ignorance and intellectual arrogance for truth.

Nine years ago, quite by accident, I stumbled upon teachings of the early Church Fathers and competent historians of the primitive Christian faith. It was during this time that I discovered my position, as an apologist for the Roman Catholic Church, was not only uninformed but that this total ignorance of Christian history was dangerous to my spiritual health as well.

Throughout these past nine years I have searched relentlessly through the writings of the early Church Fathers, along with historical accounts of the first years of Christianity. Because of this concentrated study I (as countless others through the centuries) have come to the inescapable conclusion that the doctrine of papal infallibility and supreme jurisdiction is not only in direct contradiction to Sacred Scripture and Christian tradition, but a teaching which clearly flirts with blasphemy itself! These seemingly harsh words come from a man who felt the scales fall from his eyes and experienced the spirit of truth inhabit his soul as he sought the primitive, untouched teachings of our Lord Jesus Christ and the expressed will of Almighty God.

"The Lord said to Paul, 'Go because I have chosen you to serve me, to make my name known to the Gentiles and kings and to the people of Israel. And I myself will show him all that you must suffer for my sake.'

"So Ananias went, entered the house where Saul was, and placed his hands on him. 'Brother Saul,' he said, 'the Lord has sent Jesus Himself, Who appeared to you on the road as you were coming here. He sent me that you might see again and be filled with the Holy Spirit.' At once something like fish scales fell from Saul's eyes, and he was able to see again. He stood up and was baptized. After he had eaten, his strength came back." (Acts 9:15-19)

To those who might complain that I have read too much into my experiences, I can only offer the explanations which I now set forth in print. To those who might say that I am both presumptuous and proud, fighting the teachings of centuries, my only response is that over the centuries millions of other firm believers have reached the same conclusions as I, which lend credence to my claims and impel me to submit my newly-found freedom to the pure evidence of Scripture and logic along with the sure judgement of history and tradition.  And while sheer numbers may not ensure truth, sincere searching for God's will is mandated by Holy Scripture (James 5:19; John 3:21).

Upon serious reflection it occurs to me that when a Roman Catholic, schooled in the papal way, thinks of any denomination within Christianity he will automatically, as if by reflex, ask "Are you under the pope?"  A negative reply will bring silent scorn and derision by some, and only serves to underscore my contention that the papal system is not only crucial,  but at the *very core* of Roman Catholic belief and practice.  Would that millions of Roman Catholics, as did I, come to know the dangers inherent in believing that infallibility and supreme jurisdiction, so central to the Roman system of belief, are Scripturally unsound, historically untenable, and morally dangerous! Hopefully they will accept the authentic teaching of the faith that salvation comes from the acceptance of Jesus Christ as Lord and Redeemer with allegiance to *Him* personally — not to a majority vote, a universally contested dogma, or a mere creation of men.

> "For God has already placed Jesus Christ as the *one and
> only foundation,* and no other foundation can be laid."
> (I Cor 3:11)

To those who would dismiss such protestations as nonsense, may I name just a few relevant examples to substantiate my claims.  Prior to Vatican I devotion, approaching phyletism relative to the Bishop of Rome, could be seen in a prayer, published in the Roman Breviary or Prayer Book which ascribed to the pope the title "King of Kings" and "Supreme Ruler of the World."  This excessive veneration included appellations such as "Vice-God of Humanity" and "Exalted King of the Universe." The Vatican Newspaper *La Civilta Cattolica* recorded that the pope was the "Mind of God" and pontificated that "when the pope meditates, it is God Who thinks in him."  Bishop Bereaud of Tulle, France, wrote that "the pope was the Word of God made flesh, living in our midst."  Subsequently, in 1870, the Bishop of Geneva, Switzerland, Gaspare Mermillod, commented that there is a "three-fold Incarnation of Christ in the Virgin's womb, in the Holy Eucharist, and in the pope in the Vatican" (Roger Auber, *Le Pontificate de Pie IX*, Paris, 1952, p. 302; and August Hasler, *How the Pope Became Infallible:* Doubleday, 1981, pp. 47-48). The Jesuits referred to the pope as "Redeemer!" John Bosco reminded us that the pope was "God on earth" while triumphantly proclaiming that "Jesus has placed the pope higher than the prophets, than John the Baptist, and than all the angels." He concluded, to no one's surprise, that "Jesus has put the pope *on the same level as God*"! (John Bosco, *Meditazioni,* Vol. I: 2nd ed., pp. 89-90)

Such deification of the pope had been developing for centuries and climaxed in the proclamation by the Roman Catholic Church of his infallibility during the famous Vatican Council I concluded in 1870. The rather lofty declarations quoted above have never been disowned by the Vatican; therefore, they are still part of official Roman Catholic lore. Thus one can only conclude that such statements are still viewed by the Roman Church as noteworthy and true. Yet, with such profound foolishness abounding, can anyone fail to realize the conditions which brought about a declaration of infallibility in the first place? —a doctrine which is against the primitive faith, which deludes men and women, and is clearly a human perversion of divine truth!

Lord John Emmerich Acton, one of the most distinguished Roman Catholics in England at the time of Vatican Council I, respected for his integrity and spiritual values, spoke to the British Prime Minister Gladstone when the latter wrote against the decisions of the council: "I think, Sir, that you are too hard on the Ultramontanes (those in favor of infallibility)…and too gentle on Ultramontanism. You say, for instance, that it (Ultramontanism) promotes untruthfulness. I don't think that is fair. It not only promotes, it inculcates distinct mendacity and deceitfulness. In certain cases, it is made a duty to lie. But those who teach this doctrine of infallibility do not become habitual liars in other respects." (from *Lord Acton's Correspondence,* ed. by J.N. Figgis and Lawrence, p. 93)

Once more… to critics who will make light of the above references as aberrations, allow me to quote *directly* from both popes and theologians on this self-same topic:

> *Moreri (Roman theologian):*
> "To make war against the pope is to make war against God,
> seeing that the pope is God and God is the pope."

*Nicolaus de Tudeschis, in "Commentaria" (lvi, 34):*
## "The pope can do all things God can do."

*Pope Leo XIII:*
## "We hold upon this earth the place of God Almighty."
(June 20, 1894; *Great Encyclical Letters of Pope Leo XIII:* Benziger Brothers, "Reunion of Christendom", p. 304)

*Pope (St.) Pius X:*
**"The pope is not only representative of Jesus Christ, but he is Jesus Christ Himself, hidden under the veil of the flesh. Does the pope speak? It is Jesus Christ Himself Who speaks."**

Not to be outdone, *Pope Pius XI* declared:
**"You know that I am the Holy Father, the representative of God on earth, the Vicar of Christ, which means that I am God on earth."**
(Butler, *Vatican I*, Vol. I; also, *Scriptural Truths for Roman Catholics:* Dr. B. Brewer, Mission to Catholics, Int.)

Lest anyone think that things have changed from those triumphal days of the late nineteenth and early twentieth centuries, they have only to read the words uttered recently by Cardinal John O'Connor of New York:

**"The Holy Father is the *true successor of Christ* on earth."**
(Sermon, St. Patrick's Cathedral, New York, March 1987)

and until the ritual was terminated by Pope John Paul I, when the triple crown was placed on the head of a new pope at his "coronation" the officiating cardinal proclaimed:

**"Receive the tiara adorned with three crowns, and know that thou art the Father of Princes and Kings, Ruler of the World; the Vicar of Our Saviour Jesus Christ..."** *(vicar: n., a substitute)*

***the ritual changed; the words remain.***

The celebrated *New York Catechism* states clearly and proclaims, somewhat embarrassingly, that,

**"The pope takes the place of Jesus Christ on earth... the arbiter of the world, the supreme judge of heaven and earth, the judge of all, being judged by no one, God himself on earth."** (Exact Translation)

History tells us a relatively different tale!  The Bishops of Rome were quite fallible beings even when they pretended not to speak "ex cathedra". Prone to errors of judgement and capable of proclaiming personal opinions as the voice of God, it is clear from both history and tradition that only the Word of God in Holy Scripture is infallible and unchanging truth cemented by the uninterrupted spiritual witness of the Apostolic Fathers and the indefectible mind of Christ's Church.

*"All Scripture is given by inspiration of God, and is profitable for doctrine, for reproof, for correction, for instruction in righteousness; that the man of God may be perfect..."*  (II Timothy 3:16-17)

In his marvelous series *Daily Bible Studies,* one of the era's greatest Scripture scholars, William Barclay, says simply, yet with the authority of the ages:

"Jesus Christ is the real foundation of the Church, and THE ONLY POWER WHO HOLDS THE CHURCH TOGETHER.  When Jesus said to Peter that on him He would found His Church, He did not mean that the Church depended on Peter, as it depended on Himself and on God the Rock. He did mean that the Church BEGAN with Peter: in the sense that Peter is the foundation of the Church... the first of the fellowship of those who believe in My name.  What began with Peter was the fellowship of all believers in Jesus Christ, embracing all who love the Lord and read His Holy Word." *(The Gospel of St. Matthew, Vol. II)*

Roman Catholics find it hard to accept, because of intense conditioning, that their Church with its medieval trappings of power and prestige and an institution whose unique infrastructure depends on an archaic system of law could separate itself from the "purity" of the early Church.  They ask, quite sincerely, "Could so many people be deluded into following such a faulty system of belief?"  These faithful miss the point entirely.  Size has absolutely no bearing on truth, unless that truth is supported by the witness of Holy Scripture and the teachings of the apostolic faith.

We know, of course, that in His last hours Jesus was abandoned by all but a few, and without hesitation we are reminded of the teaching of St. Athanasius who said, "Even if those faithful to tradition are reduced to a handful, they are the ones who are the true Church of Jesus Christ."  (St. Athanasius, *Apology).*  This, too, is a teaching of the Roman Catholic

Church, with force of law:  refer to *Syllabus of Errors;* Pius IX, No. 60, which states: "To one who says, 'Authority is nothing else but numbers and material strength,' let him be anathema." (1864)  While the *Syllabus* is an untamed document of triumphalism, it still comes back to haunt Roman doctrine and practice!

Think well!  Are we the Church simply because of demographics, or are we the Church because we are founded and built on the teachings of the apostles and prophets?  Is one an authentic Christian because he submits to the Roman Pontiff, or because he follows Jesus in His teachings, His message and His sublime actions, irregardless of numbers?  Although statistics are usually dangerous digits, we cautiously remind those who wish to plead that mere crowds determine truth to consider that:

— There are over one billion Moslem faithful — one fifth of all humanity — in the world today *(Zwemer Institute of Moslem Studies).*  They have grown by over 235% in the last fifty years, making them the largest of the monotheistic faiths and the world's fastest growing religion.  In England today, there are as many Moslems at the mosques on Fridays as there are Christians in church on Sundays.  The United States has approximately 3.5 million Moslems (Muslims).

— There are at least half a billion sincere, atheistic Communists around the globe, while

— there are vast numbers of the human race espousing no religious affiliation at all, reciting no formal creed, and who are, in large measure, totally ignorant of the message of Jesus Christ.


You see, if one wishes to play a "numbers game" with God, by saying that seven hundred million Roman Catholics (many nominal) can't be wrong, then it is best to beware!  Statistics cut both ways!  Reducing truths to mere statistics or results of opinion polls is very dangerous business indeed.  Numbers simply have no bearing where truth is concerned, whereas unchanging witness to the truth counts for everything.  Consider the statement of Archbishop Daniel Pilarczyk during the 1987 visit of Pope John Paul II to the United States: "The purpose of the Church is not to have lots of people in it; the purpose is to teach the teachings of Christ." (*National Catholic Reporter,* Oct. 1987)

*"At the present time there is a small remnant left whom God has selected out of His grace." (Romans 11:5)*

This short account of the innovations of the Roman Catholic Church over the past centuries will attempt to show how the doctrines of papal infallibility and so-called "universal (supreme) jurisdiction" over all

Christians have clearly become a massive barricade to proclaiming the apostolic faith and achieving genuine Christian unity. The need to amass power at the expense of truth is an age-old temptation contrary to Biblical tradition and the witness of history. Clearly, the will of almighty God is that "All may be one" (John 17:21). But never at the expense of truth!

Hopefully, this short history will begin to make you think, pray and hope for enlightenment.

The Rev. Fr. Marc Auer<br>New York

---

"Rome insists on her "rights" and appeals to Scripture and history for verification of these claims. If one is to correct misguided souls, he must appeal first to Holy Scripture and then to history... either of which are sufficient to destroy the myth of papal supremacy."

*Time for Truth (Dec. 1986)*

---

"Pope John XXIII had, from the start, no ambition whatever of proclaiming an infallible definition. On the contrary, he continually stressed in his words and in the most varied ways his own humanity, his limitations, and now and again even his own fallibility."

(Hans Kung, *Infallibility, an Inquiry*, p. 11)

"If there is ONE THING on which Christ Himself, the apostles, and the fathers insisted, it was that the Church on earth will be reduced, (in the last days) to a very small remnant. We have been warned on the highest authority of a 'falling away', that 'the time will come when they will not endure sound doctrine' (II Tim. 4:3) and that 'the very elect will be deceived.' (Mt. 24:24)" (Fr. Hugh Ross Williamson, convert Roman Catholic priest of England)

## "Will the Son of Man find faith on earth when He comes again?"
### (Luke 18:8)

**"Laypersons have always been the enemies of the clergy,"** said Pope Boniface VIII in 1296. Clearly this was no infallible pronouncement; the theory of papal infallibility did not exist at the time."

—*Peter Hebblethwaite,*<br>National Catholic Reporter, *Oct. 16, 1987, p. 9*

While we must again remind readers that demographics can be dangerous tools indeed, a recent survey by the *National Catholic Reporter* com-
missioned as an in-depth examination of Roman Catholic *opinion* in the
United States (Sept. 11, 1987) revealed that only 26% of Roman Catholics
in this country believe in the "infallibility of the pope". This despite the fact
that over three-quarters thought well of the present pope as a media figure.
Obviously, while Rome basks in the numbers of her "faithful", few of those
faithful believe what she teaches.

"You are not the Lord of Bishops, simply one of their number."
*Bernard of Clairvaux to Pope Eugene III (1145-1153)*


"People are often bewildered by the conflicting claims of the various
Churches and the disappointing conduct of their members. Particularly in
the spiritual realm a state of uncertainty is a state of misery:  so the Roman
Church finds the situation ideally suited to her purposes.

"People are fascinated by a Church which promises stability and calm.
If the priest or Church says a thing is suitable, then it is suitable; their
consciences are relieved since they do not have to make a particular
judgement on their own.

"The doctrine of infallibility appeals to many people who are poorly
informed or who are adrift spiritually.  These people know practically
nothing about the Bible.  Consequently they have no sound theology on
which to base their actions.

"They tend to surrender without first examining the promised certainty,
only to find after it is too late that they have been cruelly deceived and that
they cannot surrender their consciences to the rule of any man or Church."
—Loraine Boettner, *Roman Catholicism,* p. 238


"We are therefore disposed with great tolerance towards Roman
Catholics who believe in the divine origin of the papal prerogatives; for we
know that this prejudgement is communicated to all of them with the first
elements of religious instruction, and that everything in the Roman Church
tends to strengthen it in their souls.

"But the more deeply rooted is this delusion... the more are we bound
to dispute it with vigor."

Abbé Guettée, D.D. (1866),
Roman Catholic historian and author

**Lift up your voice like a trumpet and show the people their transgressions and the house of Jacob their sins.** (Isaiah 58:1)

The pronouncement of the Roman Catholic fold to be the "one, true Church," to which every man and woman must belong to achieve salvation, is based solely upon the belief that the papacy is divinely-mandated and the only foundation of Christ's kingdom on earth. However, if this claim to supremacy in religious and moral matters, this universal jurisdiction over mankind, fails, then the entire infrastructure of the Roman Church is affected as a result.

Most Roman Catholics think of the papacy as something which was established by Jesus Christ Himself. They innocently believe, as they have been taught by their Church since childhood, that the papacy was simply handed intact to St. Peter by Christ in the earliest days of the Christian era. Of course, to the serious student of religion this claim is without the slightest foundation in either history or Scripture, and all but the most biased narratives of Roman claims must include within their pages certain factual accounts regarding the origin and subsequent growth of the papacy which will most certainly prove any supposition to be patently false.

A few of the most important and salient historical developments are presented on these pages as proof that, although Rome held a position of lofty respect in the early days of Christianity, the doctrine of papal infallibility is of very recent origin and was, in fact, vehemently denied by both popes and faithful laymen for almost nineteen centuries—that is, before the massive "Ultramontane" movement of the mid-1800's sought to concentrate supreme religious power in the popes and the curia at Rome and prior to the Vatican Council of 1870 which proclaimed for all time the "certain infallibility" of the bishop of that place.

## EARLIEST EVIDENCE: PETER AS ROCK?

The infallibilist's view of the papacy is based on the so-called "Petrine Theory": namely, that Peter as first Bishop of Rome transmitted his "divinely-given office" to future bishops of that city so they might serve as an ultimate source of authority in the Church. So doing, say the Romanists, St. Peter handed over his role as Vicar of Christ, "successor" of the Lord Himself, to future popes whoever they might be. Rome insists that this is the definition of Peter as "Rock", yet we will see that this is not so.

Even to the most casual observer it is obvious that the earliest Christian tradition points to St. Paul and St. Peter as joint witnesses to a Church at Rome which was founded by anonymous Christians years before St. Paul arrived in the capital city. (Historians are still divided as to whether, or at what time, Peter arrived there.) It is also known that the resting places of both martyrs are mentioned by the Roman presbyter Gaius about the year 200.

"Gaius has this to say about the places where the mortal remains of the two apostles have been reverently laid:

"I can point out the monuments of the victorious apostles. If you will go out as far as the Vatican or Ostian Way, you will find the monuments of those who witnessed in this Church." (Eusebius, *History of the Church,* p. 105)

Now if this is fact, one can only wonder why St. Paul is so overshadowed as a witness of the Church at Rome? While we may never fully understand the rationale for this historical lacuna, we must keep in mind that Paul's mission was to the Gentiles (e.g., those at Rome), and Peter's was to the Jews. This occasioned a number of contributing factors which may have caused the lengthening shadows over Paul's contributions to the Christian community in the Eternal City.

For the first three centuries of Christian history the Bishop of Rome, whoever he was at the time, issued decrees in the name of "Paul and Peter". It was only with the pontificates of Callistus (217-222) and Stephanus (254-257) that Roman bishops began to compute their succession from Peter alone. Therefore the Roman claim to be the "See of Peter" can be traced at the earliest to the fourth century, and not to the most ancient period of the faith. Obviously, Paul was slowly given tertiary status to enhance Peter's role, to center authority in a local Church by appealing to the need for "one voice" in ecclesiastical affairs, a strategy prompted and propagated by a simple lust for power. However, this attempt at achieving hegemony was long in coming, since it is an historical and indisputable fact that the bishops of Rome continued to issue formal declarations in the names of both apostles, so dear to the Roman Church, until the ninth century, at which time the custom of proclaiming rescripts in Peter's name alone was conveniently initiated by Pope Nicholas I. Clearly, theory and practice regarding Peter's unique status of "first pope" were not in tandem until the early Medieval period.

We wonder aloud at St. Paul's descent in relation to the Roman community since Scripture is definite in stating that St. Peter, although a leader of the apostles in the earliest days (he was called the "chorus leader" in some documents), could not have been the monarchical bishop claimed by Rome today. This in light of the fact that Peter speaks to the college of apostles residing at Jerusalem in a most revealingly precise manner:

"I who am *an elder myself,* appeal to the Church LEADERS among you. I am a witness of Christ's sufferings and I will SHARE the glory to be revealed. *I appeal* to all of you, be shepherds of the flock that God gave you and take care of it willingly. And when Christ the Chief Shepherd appears you will receive the glorious crown." (I Peter 5:1) Peter seems to be almost begging the elders for equanimity, stressing that he too should be accepted by the Church. "I who am an elder myself appeal to you..."

St. Paul says much the same thing in Acts, Chapter 20, when he writes to the elders at Ephesus:

"Be on guard for yourselves and all your flock among which the Holy Spirit has made you overseers, to shepherd the Church of God which He purchased with His own blood... Fierce wolves will come upon the flock and tell lies to the believers."

Therefore, it can be clearly discerned from these corresponding passages that Paul, as well as Peter, taught, appealed and exhorted the elders to share in the ministry and be faithful witnesses of Christ's death and resurrection. This is even more evident when we realize that both Paul and Peter had to gain the recognition and approval of the parent Church at Jerusalem before their converts could be admitted as full members of the faith. Peter, especially, found opposition swirling around him...

"When Peter came up to Jerusalem, those who were circumcised took issue with him... (regarding converts). Peter began to explain his actions to them... and when they heard (Peter's explanation) they quieted down and glorified God." (Acts 11)

Roman apologists make much of Peter's exalted position, yet it is clear from Scripture that Peter had to justify his actions before the Church and later was confronted "to his face" by those who felt he was doing wrong. Clearly, no "papal supremacy" here! (Galatians, chapter 2) One sees in these practices a difficulty with interpreting status versus jurisdiction in the early Church. Oscar Cullman, among the most honored historians in the faith, discusses just this problem in his distinguished work, *Peter: Disciple, Apostle, Martyr:*

"Peter played a significant role in the primitive Church... however, as soon as a foundation for leadership is laid, Peter gives up this role. Another, James (brother of the Lord), will take over leadership in Jerusalem while Peter will concentrate entirely on his missionary work and will do so, indeed, in a subordinate role under James."

In *Ecclesiastical History* (II, 23,4) Eusebius, an early historian, quoting Hegesippus an eye-witness, relates concisely, yet forcefully:

**"The brother of the Lord, James, took over leadership of the Church with the apostles when control passed to them."**

Meanwhile, Cullman's extensive research into rare and early documents, even fraudulent papers such as the "Clementina", state: "Very important is the fact that the *Pseudo-Clementina,* which are (generally) favorable to Peter, clearly subordinate Peter to James... In them, Peter has to 'give an accounting to James, the bishop of the holy Church.' Subsequently, Peter sends his public address to him and Clement, using rare speech, calls James 'bishop of bishops... leader of the holy Church of the Hebrews and of the Churches founded everywhere by God's providence.' Clement traces Peter's commission back to a command that James gave to Peter. These late reports thus agree with what we can learn concerning James from the letters of Paul and the Book of Acts." (O. Cullman, *Peter: Disciple, Apostle, Martyr)*

Of course, in handing over his shared leadership role to James in order to become a missionary, Peter is dependent on the synod of Churchmen in Jerusalem, and is quite careful to guard his actions in Antioch since he has to "fear the people who come from James." (Galatians 2:12)

Obviously, Peter was doing things in Antioch proscribed by Jerusalem, such as "eating with the Gentiles," prior to the coming of "certain men from James." Afterward, "he began to withdraw and hold himself aloof, fearing the party of the circumcision," prompting Paul to speak of Peter's "hypocrisy". (Galatians 2:13) Add to these facts the clear reference in Scripture that Jesus firmly refused to give any of his disciples a position of *complete authority* (e.g., who would be the greatest or most favored), and we have an almost total absence of evidence that Christ gave roles of supremacy or sole jurisdiction over the Church to Peter or any other apostle. Leadership roles, yes; supremacy, no!


**"An argument broke out among the disciples as to which one of them should be thought of as the greatest. Jesus said to them, 'The kings of the pagans have power over their people, and the rulers are called Friends of the People. But this is not the way it is with you: rather, the greatest one among you must be like the youngest, and the leaders must be like the servants."** (Luke 22:24-27)


"Then James and John... came to Jesus. 'Teacher,' they said, 'there is something we want you to do for us.' 'What is it?' Jesus asked them.

"They answered, 'When you sit on your throne in your glorious Kingdom, we want you to let us sit with you, one on your left and one on your right.'

'You do not know what you are asking,' said Jesus. 'Can you drink the cup of suffering that I must drink? Can you be baptized in the way I must be baptized?'

**"Jesus called all the disciples together. He said, 'You know that the men who are considered rulers of the heathen have power over them, and the leaders have *complete authority*. This, however, is not the way it is with you."** (Mark 10:35-45)

Of course, the logical question in regard to such disputes is that if we accept the Roman view that Christ did grant complete authority to Peter alone (which He did not) in Matthew 16, and the apostles certainly knew this, why did they find it necessary to quiz Christ on this very matter a short time later in Matthew 18:1?

In Matthew, "The disciples asked Jesus... who is the greatest in the kingdom?" and obviously received a polite answer since we see clearly in the Book of Acts (chapter 15:6, 22-23) that a polity of authority had already been established within the early Church:

"The apostles and the elders met together to consider the question... Peter spoke, then James... with the final decision being made by the apostles, and the elders with the whole Church" (v. 22). ("Elders" were officials of various missions and Churches in diaspora.)

Again, it is easily perceptible from Scripture that no apostle or elder was to exercise complete jurisdictional control over the Church from the onset of its history. Couple this evidence with Peter's refusal of any honor when he was greeted as a god by Cornelius:

"Stand up... I myself am only a man." (Acts 10: 25-26), and one can readily comprehend that Peter, although an apostle of charisma and renown and the spokesman for a mission to the Jews, imparted no special placement to himself, and had to sit in council with the others in order to make fundamental decisions for the infant Church, judgements not made hastily, but under the guidance of the Holy Spirit within an aura of fraternity and consultation.

It would be enough for some to end here, for Scripture is confidently on the side of those who make no special claims for the papacy and see the desire for "infallibility" as a basic human urge for power, hegemony and triumphalism — inherent in an innate quest for security and stability. Nevertheless, we shall go on.

# Was Peter the Rock: The Foundation of the Church?

Rome proudly declares to us that St. Peter is the ROCK upon which Christ wished to build His Church. In confronting this claim one must understand the language of Scripture and the syntax of Biblical Greek, while realizing that the inflated position of Rome is precariously grounded in one hotly-disputed passage of Holy Scripture. This passage allegedly bequeaths Christianity's prime leadership role solely to the Bishop of Rome, for all time and people.

The Scriptural quotation, the famous and controversial statement of Peter's alleged "supreme jurisdiction", is found in Matthew 16:15-20.

"He said to them, 'But who do you say that I am?'

"And Simon.Peter answered and said, 'Thou art the Christ, the Son of the living God.'

"And Jesus answered and said to him, 'Blessed are you, Simon Bar-Jonah, because flesh and blood did not reveal this to you, but My Father Who is in heaven.

"'And I say to you that you are Peter (petros), and upon this Rock (petra) I will build My Church; and the gates of Hell shall not overpower it.

"'I will give you the keys of the kingdom of heaven; and whatever you shall bind on earth shall have been bound in heaven, and whatever you shall loose on earth shall have been loosed in heaven.'

"Then He warned them that they should tell no one that He was the Christ."

The Greek equivalent for Peter is *petros* meaning "little stone". The Greek word for Rock is *petra*. *Petra* is feminine; therefore it could not refer to a masculine Peter (a fact conveniently overlooked by Roman apologists). Therefore, what Jesus actually said is:

"YOU ARE PETER (*petros* — a little stone) AND UPON THIS ROCK (*petra* — your proclamation of me as Christ) I WILL BUILD MY CHURCH, since you alone could not support the weight of its foundation."

In other words, Jesus will build His Church upon a person's profession of faith in Him as the Christ — not on a mere mortal man such as Peter. Sure resolution of this problem certainly lies in the appropriate definition of the term "ROCK".

St. Paul answers this question for us. He states, without qualification, that CHRIST IS THE ROCK! (I Corinthians 3:11)

"For no man can lay a foundation other than the one which is laid, which is JESUS CHRIST."

Christ never proclaimed that He would build His Church on a man (Peter), a "little stone", that would be too faulty a foundation. He would build His Church on Himself, the only foundation possible, and on Peter's profession of faith *(homologica)* which is, coincidentally, feminine in Greek and corresponds exactly to *petra,* a large, unmoveable monolith!

Obviously, the apostle himself recognizes these facts and in I Peter (2: 5-8) he speaks of believers as "stones", and of Jesus as the Rock "upon which God builds." Even that great scholar of the early Church, St. Cyril, in his *Fourth Book on the Trinity,* states unambiguously,

"I know that by Rock you must understand the unshakeable faith of the apostles in Christ."

In concert with this, Saint Hilary says in his *Sixth Book on the Trinity:*

"The Rock *(petra)* is the blessed and only Rock of the faith which is confessed by the mouth of Peter; 'Thou art the Christ, the Son of the living God.'" This learned saint continues, "It is on this Rock of confession of faith that the Church is built,"

while no less a personality than St. John Chrysostom, certainly a definite friend of episcopal oversight, proclaims:

"The Rock on which Christ will build His Church means the *faith of confession."* (from the *Homilies*)

Doubtless the early Church had no knowledge of a doctrine invented centuries later, by partisans of the Roman cause, which spoke of the Rock as the person of Peter! Additionally, we can safely state that it is purely arbitrary, and an act of historical bravado, to insist that Christ built His Church upon St. Peter solely as a "place, where, on a certain date, this or that Church was the leader of Christendom." (Cullman, *op. cit.,* p. 236) The Church of Christ is much too all-embracing and expansive to be limited to a particular time, place or person!

Since Christ refused to impart supreme authority or jurisdiction to any single member of the apostolic community, it is crucial to remember that IF Christ had determined that a superior position was to be given to Peter, and IF He had granted a more lofty place to him than to the others — would Jesus have said to Peter that the twelve apostles should be seated upon the twelve thrones of the kingdom without distinction of honor? (Mark 3:13-15, and Matthew 19:28)

After the ascension of the Lord, Peter appeared as a spokesman for the apostolic band — as he often did during the earthly life of Jesus. "Go tell his disciples and Peter," the angel commanded at the tomb (Mark 16:7). However, aside from Peter's role as a spokesman (Gk: *coryphæus*) and his bold witness of Christ's divinity, there is not one shred of evidence that he possessed any supremacy OVER the others, let alone that he was endowed with the promise of infallibility. We have seen Peter's part as spokesman, which he relinquished to James, and we know that he was the prototype of a Christian by his confession of faith at Cæsarea Philippi. Subsequently, we believe it was Peter's role to provide an example to all believers for all times, to teach, to speak, and to witness to the Lord.

Assigning Peter an exclusive role as "keeper of the keys of the Kingdom" flies in the face of all relevant testimony which imparts the power of "binding and loosing of sins" to each apostle (Matthew 18:18), as an occupant of the twelve thrones (Luke 22:30). Add to this the clear mandate of the fourth Gospel (John) naming the only "representative" of the risen and glorified Lord, the true "Vicar of Christ" on earth, i.e., the Paraclete, the Holy Spirit (John 16:13) and one is certainly able to determine the essential role played by the college of the apostles in the primitive Church. Christ has already sent the leader of His flock, the Holy Spirit; therefore, we have no need for human "vicars". We have a divine master in the Paraclete.

Once again we are reminded of the observation made by Origen in the early third century: "If we also say, Thou art the Christ, the Son of the living God, then we also become Peter...for whoever assimilates to Christ, becomes the Rock. Does Christ give the keys of the Kingdom to Peter alone, whereas other blessed people cannot receive them?" *(Homily on Matthew, XII, x)*

Even Thomas Aquinas, the greatest theologian of the Roman Church, teaches that while the promise of indefectability does not exempt individual Christians from susceptibility to error, it does promise the guidance of the Holy Spirit. This very special protection of the Paraclete works well in shielding one from "wandering" when reflecting on "the truths of the faith." (ThAq 2a, 2ae, 1:3; 8:4a, d; 1:2 ad, d. *Summa*)

In his thorough study, *Towards Christian Reunion,* Luis Bermejo, S.J., comments:

"Just as the promise of the indwelling of the Spirit cannot be restricted to the eye-witnesses (i.e., apostles) but extends to all future disciples, so also the promise of the Spirit's guidance into the fulness of truth goes well beyond the restricted circle of the Twelve." Venturing then into a critical, yet controversial, area, Fr. Bermejo concludes that "This promise is probably an answer to the anxiety and even skepticism caused by the delay of Jesus' return."

In much the same vein, Raymond Brown, Roman Catholic priest and Church historian, concludes that:

"The Christian need not live with his eyes constantly straining towards heaven from which the Son of Man is to come, for, as the Paraclete, Jesus is present within all believers." (R. Brown, *The Gospel According to John*, p. 137)

## "FOR AS MANY AS ARE LED BY THE SPIRIT OF GOD, THESE ARE THE SONS OF GOD."
### (Romans 8:14)

**"Where the Church is, there is the Spirit of God: and where the Spirit of God is, there is the Church, and every kind of grace; but the Spirit is truth."**

— Irenæus, *Against Heresies*, iii, 24

"At that time the *Disciples* came to Jesus... (He said), 'Truly I say to you, whatever you shall bind on earth shall have been bound in heaven; and whatever you loose on earth shall be loosed in heaven... If two of you agree on earth about anything that they might ask, it shall be done for them by My Father in heaven." (Matthew 18:1 and 18-20)

In addressing the assembled Church, not Peter alone, Jesus taught the believers these things immediately before His death:

"But the Helper, the Holy Spirit, Whom the Father will send in My name, He will teach you all things, and bring to your remembrance all that I said to you." (John 14:26)

"I have many more things to say to you, but you cannot hear them now. *But when He, the Spirit of truth, comes, He will guide you into all the truth; for He will not speak on His own initiative, but whatever He hears He will speak; and He will disclose to you what is to come.* He shall glorify Me, for He shall take of Mine, and shall disclose it to you." (John 16: 12-14)

After gleaning passages such as these, one can only conclude that there is nothing here of a papal "comforter", an infallible bishop, or a supreme human teacher! Had Jesus wished to assign such a role to the Bishop of Rome, He would not have deceived us so cruelly by promising to send the "Paraclete... to teach you all things... to guide you into all the truth," when it was the pope He intended to provide for our solace and direction.

Within these passages the New Testament undeniably promises each believer that the all-pervading presence of the Holy Spirit will guide Christians to the truth. Nothing here of pontiff or curia being the exclusive heirs to the "truth and promise" as they claim. This binding guarantee of guidance applies to every Christian and not just those "divinely revealed dogmas" spoken of in encyclicals and rescripts, reserved to popes and cardinals, committed to "load the backs" of the faithful with "man-made laws" (Matthew 23).

As for the argument that Church order demands a single, central authority be developed and nurtured to "help" believers interpret Holy Scripture, one can only think of truth found in the venerable Orthodox Church which by her very nature relies on the decentralization of human authority and calls calmly upon the Holy Spirit, each time she prays, to help her leaders "rightly divide the word of Your truth," thus setting an example of total reliance upon the Paraclete, our surety of faith.

In support of this basic truth, inherent in the Church by her mission to teach all men in all ages, we turn to the writings of Dr. Hans von Campenhausen who succinctly records the role of order and leadership in the early Christian community.

"(Until the fifth century) there was certainly no talk about the primacy of those who bore (Church) office. They indeed, by their office, were called and empowered to interpret Scripture, and represented, in virtue of their commission, the original Apostolic truth... but one bishop was not made 'lord of Scripture' and had no exclusive right or privilege of knowing and deciding what it really meant. Not only was the right of 'private use of Scripture' taken for granted all through ecclesiastical antiquity; even the leading theologians were laymen."

Dr. von Campenhausen, called an expert in the finest sense of the word, has devoted a lifetime to finding out what the primitive Church was really like. In his famous work, *Tradition and Life in the Church,* he concludes:

"Throughout the early period of the Church there was only one authority which — beginning in the third century — raised the unheard-of claim, on the basis of a supposed scriptural and irrefutable right, to be able to ascertain the truth with certainty, to expound and establish it, over and above anyone else. This was the Roman Pontiff, in his papal authority as asserted and formulated by, for example, Leo the Great, about the middle of the fifth century. Then there was developed, in opposition to this, a correspondingly absolute and exclusive conciliar theory, which, owing to political complications, could not be made to prevail. The nature of these endeavors reveals their fatal intention of making the Church secure through a definite order of domination, though this became evident only in the high and later Middle Ages, when the authority of the pope turned and established itself against the 'unauthorized' appeal to Holy Scripture. Thus the idea of a supposed God-given sacred order of the Church became, in fact, the mortal enemy of its true life, whose source was the Word of God."

Clearly, by this point in our study it should be quite obvious that if a person (opting for the truth and open to what might be shattering arguments against his *a priori* opinions), consulted those well schooled in early Church history, he must stand ready to confront almost universal agreement AGAINST any innovation which makes ONE bishop of the Church supreme in matters of jurisdiction, or which empowers him to unilaterally interpret Holy Scripture for the entire Church. This is precisely because there is not one unbiased historian worth his salt who will, based on years of exhaustive study, support the theory of "infallibility". Of course this excludes ecclesiastical apologists who approach such investigation attempting to prove a certain point of view or official doctrine through manipulation of history and tradition. Certainly we know that any theologian who wishes to remain within the Roman Catholic tradition dare not deny papal infallibility and remain a "Catholic theologian". Witness for example Hans Kung of Germany and Charles Curran of the United States, who were recently stripped of their licenses for just such a blatant act of disloyalty and overt questioning of the official Church teaching pertaining to papal authority.

In the opinion of J. Blank, in his study of Pope Pius IX, *"Una Sancta" (33, 1978, p. 78):*

**"No reputable Catholic exegete can hold that the New Testament gives any clear support for papal primacy and infallibility. The proof from Scripture upon which the dogma was based at that time cannot be held valid today. The same is true of the proof from tradition."**

Throughout its defense of papal infallibility, Roman Catholic teaching exalts Peter's position as an apostle in relation to other early Christian teachers. Certainly Peter's position vis-a-vis Paul is noteworthy, yet as we peruse the pages of the New Testament we find no such evidence that Peter was Paul's superior in any sense — quite the contrary. We accept that Peter may be the prototype of a believer, yes, but not superior in faith to Paul the apostle. Consequently, Church Fathers knew well that Paul rebuked Peter sternly and publicly, and as a result Peter turned from his erring ways because of Paul's correction. Recognizing the conflict between these two powerful figures, early leaders such as St. John Chrysostom in his *Homily on Galatians 2:1*, and St. Jerome's *Epistles 86-97* and *Commentary on Galatians* tried to explain away any obvious rift between Peter and Paul so as not to dilute the Christian message for unbelievers. Nevertheless, the following significant passage from Holy Scripture proves again that from the earliest days "no one can speak of a primacy of Peter, except in his role as a witness within the Church" — and certainly nothing comparable to that claimed today by the Bishop of Rome." (Cullman, *Peter,* pp. 46-47.)

**"But when Peter (Cephas) came to Antioch, I opposed him to his face, because he stood condemned... And the rest of the Jews joined him (Peter) in hypocrisy."**

— Galatians 2:11-13

On the contrary, when the "apostles who were at Jerusalem" heard that Samaria had received the Word of God *they* sent both Peter and John to "that Church". (Acts 8:14) Peter was simply another member of the council of elders, albeit an exalted member, since he obeyed a representative command of the Church. Yet he had to endure a "dressing down" for his actions in feasting with uncircumcised converts (Acts 11:2-4). Would this reproach by the Church be the fate of a supreme ruler? Peter did a good thing for the faith, but was called for an accounting. Obviously, the other elders did not view him as infallible, the foundation or Rock of the Church, as proclaimed by the Romanists. The elders/apostles acted as a community in making decisions jointly, and we are reminded that although the Church may have begun with Peter's profession of faith, it obviously did not depend on Peter's "supreme jurisdiction" for survival.

Ο ΠΕΤΡΟΣ
Ο ΠΑΥΛΟΣ

Even the most cursory reading of the Book of Acts would indicate immediately that the famous Council of Jerusalem (Acts 15), the first in the Church, was presided over by James, "the brother of the Lord," the Bishop of Jerusalem — not Peter. As an apostle Peter could not lead here because he was so often absent from the city. However, St. James, not an apostle, resided in the Holy City — the birthplace of Christianity. When a decision had to be made as to whether Gentile Christians were to be circumcised, Peter was not asked for his single-minded decision. Instead, a council of the apostles was convened. Nevertheless, Peter did not act as chairman but participated as an equal, and listened, as James proposed a solution to the crisis (Acts 15:12-35). This was not, however, an isolated incident, since throughout the Book of Acts, an historical account of the infant Church, we come across statements such as

"James spoke, 'Listen to me, brothers...'"

"Then the apostles and the elders, together with the whole Church, decided..."

"We the apostles and elders send greetings..."


For some Easterners (including the historian Eusebius) St. James, not Peter, was pre-eminent as a bishop, "brother of Christ," who received the episcopate at Jerusalem "from the Savior and the apostles." Respect for the Roman See, as Origen shows, was connected solely with its "antiquity" and perhaps also with the primacy of the city of Rome as capital of the empire. (Eusebius, HE, vii; 14:10)

Eusebius, also a bishop, is not only in a superb position to judge the organization of the nascent Church, but is thoroughly supportive of the hierarchy's unique and intact role as the point of focus in post-resurrectional times. Contemporary historians, too, see startling evidence in early documents that the status claimed for Peter as some sort of super-bishop is just not there! This was a very late development pursued by ambitious Roman clerics. T.H. Klauser in *Gesammelte Arbeiten* suspects that while the names of most of the earliest Roman bishops are definitely historical, their dating is worthless. Klauser also shows, after reams of research, that "apostolic succession" is clearly shown by the earliest witnesses to be, not merely a physical laying of hands, as proponents of the Petrine Theory hold, but the *handing down of the apostolic faith* enjoined *by the imposition of hands!* (This is the exact position of the Orthodox Church to this day.) St. Paul, lacking a "physical succession", having only the direct commission of Christ, emphasizes this teaching when he exhorts the Corinthians to accept him as both an apostle and theologian.

"I do not think that I am the least bit inferior to those very special apostles of yours." (II Cor 11:5)

We know that in St. John's Gospel the disciples are often portrayed as the models for all Christians, everywhere, and at every time. What John sees and understands about the disciples, he understands about the Church.

It is the unquestioned duty of the Church to hand on the apostolic kerygma and maintain a sure fidelity to the message and teachings of the apostles without innovation or change. However, it is far from certain that the so-called "power of the keys" was viewed by the early Church in precisely the same manner, in all places. In fact, Bermejo states:

"There are traces in Paul that seem to indicate a certain reserve, if not open rejection of that authority..." (i.e., power of the keys) which some claim for Peter, and which was later formulated by the Roman Church. In an article in *Concilium* (March, 1973) on the office of Peter in the New Testament, J. Blank concludes:

"Paul recognized Peter's authority (in some ways) though in a sense of *auctoritas*, not of *potestas.*"

Paul subsequently names James first when referring to the "pillars of the Church" (Galatians 2:7-9). To him, the *leaders* of the Church (and notice the plural) "were James, Peter and John," certainly not Peter alone. Paul, as we have seen, had a mission to the Gentiles; Peter's was to the Jews, and Peter became the spokesman representing the apostles to the Chosen People. Had Peter possessed an all-encompassing jurisdiction, it would have been to Gentile and Jew alike. Logically, then, if there were to be any missionary "bishop" to Rome, a Gentile city *par excellence*, it would have most certainly evolved to Paul. To make Rome the center of the faith, and ascribe to its bishop a universal jurisdictional role, can be logically frightful as well as historically untrue.

The infant Church obviously enjoyed a profound sense of community and conciliarity, along with possessing a zealous band of missionary servants. Peter was assigned leadership of one such coterie, Paul another, both sent out by the Church under the inspiration of the Spirit. "So being sent out by the Holy Spirit, they went down to Seleucia and from there to Cyprus" (Acts 13:4). After Paul founded a number of Churches throughout the Middle East, he eventually found his way to the Imperial City, Rome (Acts 28). Peter, on the other hand, resided for some time at Antioch, about 300 miles from Jerusalem, a center for early missionary activity in the Church. As to whether Peter ever reached Rome, Scripture is strangely silent. Regardless, scholars have debated the issue for decades with arguments raging on both sides. Relating to whether he enjoyed the "jurisdictional primacy", and how so in light of such relationships, Church historians are certain. Oscar Cullman, in *Peter: Disciple, Apostle, Martyr,* concludes:

"In the time of Peter the Roman Church had no more significance, and perhaps even less, than the Church at Antioch. They were both local Churches, and as such they were led by Peter, IF the traditions in question are correct.

If one were determined to maintain the completely arbitrary principle by which Peter's episcopal office in a Church could aid in giving later bishops an exclusive claim to St. Matthew 16:17ff, then on this basis Antioch could establish *claim to primacy than Rome.*"

Thus logic once again rears honed edges able to cut both ways. If, as the Romanists maintain, it is only logical that Peter, as Bishop of Rome, received the primacy (definitely not an historical *fact*), then why can't the Antiochian party, bolstered by literary support and historical evidence, rightly maintain that Peter's episcopacy there (a witness found in both Scripture and history) established primacy for that Church?

Subsequently, in confronting these axioms, Cullman expands his theory while debasing a need for amassing power and "legitimacy" at the expense of Gospel truth.

"There is no basis whatever in any ancient text for the assertion that Rome inherited the legal succession from Jerusalem. Even if Antioch could be inserted as an intermediate stage, such a theory could not be any better supported." (Cullman, *ibid.*)

Graciously allowing for the fact that Peter did reach Rome and died there (I Clement 5:1-6:1), it is clear that there are simply no early traditions, nor documents, purporting that he ever served as "bishop-presbyter, a possibility which seems unlikely since apostles played a unique role, superior to that of local Church supervisors." (*Harper's Bible Dictionary,* p. 778, in an article by Dr. Pheme Perkins)

Raymond Brown, Roman priest and Church historian, writes:

"We have no accurate knowledge of Paul's relation to Rome between the imprisonment and the time of his death. As for Peter, we have no knowledge at all of when he came to Rome and just what he did there before he was martyred. Certainly, he was not the original missionary who brought Christianity to Rome, and therefore was not the founder of the Church of

Rome in that sense. There is no proof that he was the bishop (or local ecclesiastical officer) of the Roman Church — a claim not made... (by Rome) ...until the third century. Most likely he did not spend any major time in Rome before 58 A.D. ... and came to the capital shortly before his martyrdom." *(Antioch and Rome, p. 98)*

A tradition which is supported generously by documentation comprehends Linus as the first bishop-presbyter of Rome "consecrated" by Paul for service in that city. This is affirmed by St. Irenæus, a resident of Rome for many years (Irenæus III:23). St. Dionysius, a Christian of Corinth, credits the "founding" of the Church at Rome to both Paul and Peter. However, the word founding is a misnomer since Scripture claims that "others" founded that Church while Paul and Peter simply "witnessed" to this foundation and strengthened its resolve.

"My ambition has always been to proclaim the Good News in places where Christ had not been heard of, so as not to build on a foundation laid by someone else" (Paul to Romans, 15:20).

Paul obviously played an important, albeit absentee, role in the life of the assembly at Rome. In his famous letter to that Church he expresses great fondness and filial concern for its members, while praying for the day when he will be able to meet them personally. Eventually a spurious tradition of the Roman Church, certainly historically false, claimed Peter was bishop there for 25 years despite (Scriptural) witness that Paul in his letter (to the Roman Church) never once mentions Peter! Paul greets many faithful there, but never names Peter, which proves that the latter was not in Rome, as the papacy maintains, when he was supposed to be! (Romans 16:1-27)

Raymond Brown asserts:

"Although Rome was not a Pauline Church, evidently his letter to the Romans was well enough received to make the majority of Roman Christians recognize Paul's claim to be an apostle comparable to Peter."

In fact, Father Brown echos much of the most recent research into the early history of the Roman Church:

"The significant failure of Ignatius (c. 110) to mention the single-bishop in his letter to the Romans..., the usage of Hermas which speaks of plural presbyters (Vis 2.4.2) and bishops (Sim. 9.27.2) make it likely that a single-bishop structure did not come to Rome until c. 140-150. ...The earliest names in the Roman episcopal lists probably represent the more famous presbyter-bishops of the first hundred years of Roman Christianity, some of them functioning simultaneously." *(Antioch and Rome, pp. 163–64)*

As we have seen, Paul considered his ministry not the least bit inferior to the "others" (Galatians 2:11), and took upon himself the work of teaching the Church at Rome, founded much earlier and definitely by others, quite some time before his arrival there. Historian Hans von Campenhausen wonders aloud at such a circumstance when he inquires how this all-encompassing role of Paul's devotion to the faithful at Rome has been so "woefully" neglected and eclipsed. To him it is a most "compelling" issue! (See von Campenhausen: Chadwick; *Jerusalem and Rome.*)

As a final comment on this matter, we must not overlook the classic work on Peter by D. W. O'Connor, who places this issue in historical perspective when he concludes that:

"Nothing can be *finally* determined however about *when* Peter came to Rome, *how long* he stayed, or *what* function or leadership, if any, he exercised within the Roman Church," (D. W. O'Connor, *Peter in Rome,* p. 98) a point which Raymond Brown calls "excellent judgment." (*Antioch and Rome,* p. 98)

An interesting sidelight to this whole question is that in the earliest extant copies of the Liturgy one finds the following:
**"We make offering for Zion (Jerusalem) the Mother of All Churches,"** while the First Council of Constantinople proclaims: **"Jerusalem is the mother of all Churches."**

---

## THE OFFICE OF BISHOP AND THE BISHOP OF ROME

Undoubtedly a "given" in Church history is that, without exception, the early Fathers taught that *all* bishops or elders were direct successors of the apostles. When Sts. Cyprian, Jerome and Augustine speak of the "Chair of Peter" they mean, not the Roman See, but the *episcopal office in general* and then an office of service not jurisdiction.

It is interesting to observe how many Roman Catholic bishops and theologians of recent vintage have come to accept this definition of the role and office of bishops — each of whom by his episcopal function occupies the "Chair of Peter" — as a ministry of service, not power. Two noteworthy examples illustrate this contemporary trend:

### Catholic Prelate on the Primacy of the Pope

Patriarch Maximos IV Saigh in an interview with the *Divine Word News Service* in Rome stated that papal primacy need not be an obstacle to unity, but rather an aid. He felt that there are "excessive interpretations" of this doctrine…and made the point that the head of the Church is "Christ and He alone." Maximos IV was an Eastern Rite Patriarch under the jurisdiction of Rome.

"It is not proper to speak of the pope as the head of the Church," and Maximos maintains that "the foundation of the Church consists not only in Peter but in the other apostles as well." The Patriarch explained that "bishops are rulers in their own dioceses," and concluded that the primacy is only a pastoral one, "because it is a ministry, a service, a diaconate, as Pope Paul VI himself has said." (from *"The Light"*, 1982)

### Interprets Papal Primacy

The Rev. Fr. Victor L. Herbert, the outspoken and frank columnist of the *Byzantine Catholic World* of Pittsburgh, commenting on Patriarch Maximos IV Saigh's statement that "it is not proper to speak of the Roman Pontiff as the head of the Church," writes that "the doctrine of primacy is true is not doubted, but (that) its applications and ramifications over the years are according to Scriptural and Apostolic Tradition may be doubted and in fact very seriously so. The doctrine of papal primacy flourished only after the lance of schism pierced the side of Christ's Church… As a result, many rights of the bishops have been taken by the Holy See and have gained the mistaken position of being reserved by divine right to the Roman Pontiff alone." (from *"The Light"*, 1982)

*NB: It must be remembered that the term "primacy" means a place of honor, i.e., that a Church had apostolic foundations. Of course Rome, among many others, did have this beginning. Rome is an ancient Church and deserves honor on this account. However, there is a VAST difference between simple "primacy" and "infallibility/supreme jurisdiction" which the papacy claims for itself. And remember also that the two courageous statements above are from Roman Catholics, one a patriarch, the other a priest, who are constrained to mitigate their remarks by fear of reprisal from Church authority.

---

## THE BISHOP OF ROME: AN OVERVIEW

It was not until the early part of the second century that one could speak of a Bishop of Rome in the sense that we do today. About the year 300, he was given the honorary designation of "Archbishop", and until the late fourth century shared the title "Pope" with the bishops at Carthage and Alexandria, in Egypt. Later, this designation was claimed by bishops at all important ecclesiastical centers, such as Antioch in Syria. In 450, Leo I was the first Bishop of Rome to be titled "Patriarch", and he also used the appellation "Servant of the servants of God." Pope Damasus in the fourth century was the first Roman bishop to use the term "Apostolic See" in reference to his diocese, although as we have seen, bishops in other cities had been using this title for decades. The term simply meant that a bishop was in direct succession from an apostle, who founded that Church. "Apostolic See" was never the exclusive title of the Roman Church, although it was claimed particularly by that See. In any event, it was certainly never bestowed by "divine right" on the Bishop of Rome.

Dr. Nicon Patrinacos, distinguished theologian of the Orthodox Church, writes:

"The title Pope was used in the early times as an epithet for any bishop. In the East, it was confined only to the Patriarch of Alexandria…but as time went on the term "Pope" began to be restricted in the West only to the Bishop of Rome. At the Synod of Pavia in 998, the Archbishop of Milan was rebuked for calling himself "Pope", a term used in the Greek Church much the same way "Father" is used in the Western Church.

"Finally, in 1073 Pope Gregory VII formally prohibited in a Council in Rome the use of the name 'Pope' by any other bishop in the Western Church, other than the Bishop of Rome." (N. Patrinacos; *Dictionary of Greek Orthodoxy*)

Speaking within his famous and often-used text *The Early Church*, Henry Chadwick, professor of Church History at Oxford, Cambridge and the University of Chicago, considered an expert on the formative period of the Church, writes:

"Before the third century there was no call for a sustained, theoretical justification of this (Roman) leadership. All (Churches) were brethren, but the Church at Rome was accepted as only first among equals."

In the year 110, an important letter from St. Ignatius of Antioch conferred on Rome the descriptive title "the Church that presides in love in the country of the region of the Romans." But St. Ignatius is quick to point out that the term "presides in love" is a sign of *honor* for the Roman Church, not one of supreme jurisdiction over all the Churches of Christendom. And it is very important to remember that it is the Church and its *members* which Ignatius mentions, not the Bishop of the Imperial City.

From the earliest days of the Church, the Bishop of Rome had severe problems convincing other bishops of his supremacy in matters of doctrine and discipline. In every recorded case it is clearly shown that when the Bishop of Rome tried to coerce other bishops of the Church into conforming to his views, he was either soundly condemned, or had his decisions overturned, by indignant Churches through their synods of bishops.

To underscore these legitimate actions and reactions, one has simply to research the illuminating canons of the earliest Church councils. An especially enlightening passage from the Fourth Council at Chalcedon (451) states:

**"If a bishop has a contention with his Metropolitan,**
**let him carry the case to Constantinople."**

This was distasteful for pretentious bishops on the Tiber, and yet another bitter pill for Rome to swallow at a time when she arrogantly insisted that all Churches, wherever they might be, respond to her will. However, the other Churches knew their rights as bestowed upon them by Church councils. Witness Canon 6 of the First Council held at Nicæa in 325. Although it gave simple "primacy of honor" to Rome, she insisted it enjoined other Churches to respond to her will and dictates. This was not so, and conflicts ensued. Witness, too, the sixth Canon of the Council of Constantinople III (680), which declared: "Let the Throne of Constantinople WITH ROME ENJOY EQUAL PRIVILEGES! After it Alexandria, then Antioch, and then Jerusalem."

The beginning of the legal entity technically called the Pentarchy (or five major Sees), to one of which each local Church was expected to attach itself, was formalized by the Emperor Justinian in the sixth century (*Novella* 123). Rome enjoyed first honor since she was the capital of the empire; however, the others followed in equal dignity and privilege. Consequently, in view of these undeniable historical facts, one must concede (and this includes the most biased reviewer) that such a situation is hardly the stuff of which hegemony is made!

Yet even today, under the guise of false ecumenism, the Bishop of Rome insists that ALL Churches, of whatever stripe, return to her fold, whereupon she will exercise total control and jurisdiction over their affairs. This in spite of the so-called "ecumenical fervor" popular in some quarters. The preceding observation is not a mis-statement of fact. Allow us to quote directly from Vatican II and the famous *"Decree on Ecumenism"*:

"For it is through Christ's Catholic Church *alone,* which is the all-embracing means of salvation, that the fullness of the means of salvation can be obtained. It was to the apostolic college *alone,* of which Peter was the head, that we believe our Lord entrusted all the blessings of the New

Covenant, in order to establish on earth the *one Body of Christ into which ALL those should be incorporated who already belong in any way to God's People." (Decree of Ecumenism,* c. 3, "Unitatis Redintegratio" 7/21/74.)

Simply put, the only goal of the ecumenical movement for the Roman Catholic Church is the capitulation of ALL separated brethren to its fold in the name of Peter, "first apostle and pope"!

Rome appeals to history to justify her claims of supreme jurisdiction. So too can we appeal to history confident that Roman claims of hegemony based on "authentic" documentation are both dangerous and untrue.

Rome enjoys claiming that jurisdictional primacy comes to her by "divine right".  Almost as a chorus, historians and theologians such as Mansi, De Vries, Frend, Cullman, von Campenhausen (et al.) see in the famous Canon 28 of the Council of Chalcedon a "three-pronged attack on such Roman claims." In this specific Canon "Rome and Constantinople are accorded the same privileges *(isa presbeia)* and this tends to place both on an equal footing.  Constantinople is granted juridical powers, but they are restricted to the neighboring provinces and, by implication, the same is said of Rome:  and most damaging for her— the only reason the Roman primacy is mentioned is strictly political, i.e., Rome is the capital of the Empire." (Bermejo, p. 120)

We have touched briefly on a few extant historical papers.  The remainder of this thesis will concentrate on a number of authoritative texts which annihilate all claims of domination or supremacy on the part of the Roman See.

---

## Documents from the Past:  Authentic and Counterfeit

If Rome truly held the primacy from the time of Christ, and if the pope was supreme in all matters relating to the Church (at one time popes also claimed secular control over men's lives), then the ultimate and sole judge of conflicts would certainly not have been passed on by the ancient Church to others outside the jurisdiction of the Roman See.  Thus far in this study we have witnessed the power being relayed to Constantinople and the inevitable creation of a Pentarchy, yet there are other instances of Roman interference, and Church response to her meddling, which disprove any suggestion of supreme jurisdiction in ecclesiastical affairs from the earliest recorded history of the faith.  One of the first instances of this type took place in North Africa, a Church stubbornly independent and possessing a rich ecclesiastical history. Celestine, Pope of Rome, interfered in provincial, but important, business in these African congregations. His interest went unappreciated and Celestine was subsequently informed in a stern, provocative letter composed by the African bishops, filled with polite rebukes, that he was henceforth never to offer his opinion or become enmeshed in their affairs to any degree or substance:

"We earnestly implore you in the future not to admit readily for a hearing persons coming hence, nor choose to receive to your communion those who have been excommunicated by us, because Your Reverence (Celestine) will readily perceive that this has been prescribed by the Nicene Council." *(Celestine Letter II; PL 50. 422-27)*

The African bishops knew their rights. Respect and communion the papacy would receive, but "not the right of unsolicited and indiscriminate intervention" in the internal affairs of the African Church. (W.H.C. Frend, *Rise of Christianity*)

Another appropriate example of inflated arrogance on the part of the Roman bishop can be discerned in the so-called "Easter Question" of the mid-second century. In a famous religious document St. Irenæus, hierarch of Lyons, states that around 155 St. Polycarp, while on a visit to Rome, and Anicetus, bishop of that city, tried in vain to convince one another of the correctness of their respective traditions as to when and how the faithful should celebrate Pascha. As a result of this brief encounter and the ensuing contention, they eventually agreed to maintain their local customs and retain the traditional canons. All was well. However, by example, Irenæus, in his account of the conflict, wished to elucidate that the Roman bishops had no authority to issue universal decrees or unilateral opinions without a consensus of the unified Church, but should learn to live in peace with other brother bishops and Churches. (Irenæus, *In Haereses,* Lib. III, cap. iii)

Lessons learned from this confrontation were short-lived, and with this painful conflict still fresh in the Church's memory, Pope Victor of Rome, in AD 190, attempted to excommunicate all the bishops within Asia because they were celebrating Pascha (Easter) on a date different from the Western Church. Victor was strongly condemned for this autocratic decree and, as a result, his letters were simply ignored by every Church in the Greek East. Its bishops considered his actions "vainglorious" and totally "inconsistent" with the apostolic tradition of local Church autonomy.

The honored historian of the early Church, Eusebius, an intimate friend of the Emperor Constantine, records in his journal:

"Thereupon Victor, head of the Roman Church, attempted at one stroke to cut off from the common unity all the Asian dioceses, together with the neighboring Churches, on the ground of heterodoxy, and pilloried them in letters in which he announced the total excommunication of all his fellow Christians there.  But this was not to the taste of the bishops; they replied with a request that he 'would turn his mind to those things which make for peace and for unity and for love towards his neighbors.' ...We still possess the words of these men, who very sternly rebuked Victor."

Early historical documents, i.e. those dealing with the Paschal controversy under Pope Victor, traditionally viewed by Rome as incontrovertible evidence of papal primacy of jurisdiction, are being viewed by Roman Catholic historians today in a much different light.  Catholic historians acknowledge now that "these passages do not contain any clear assertion of Rome's jurisdictional primacy."  (L. Bermejo, *Toward Christian Reunion*, pp. 108-109)


Incidents such as these are noteworthy today since they emphasize that while Rome was beginning to view herself as the focus of authority within the Church, the residuum of Christianity saw the Church rather as an ellipse with the foci on both Jerusalem in the East and Rome in the West.

The views of Irenæus are also significant to heed, since in his celebrated work, *Adverses Hæreses (Against Heresies)*, composed between 180-199 A.D., he mentions the Bishop of Rome by name and enumerates exactly what his administrative role should be within the Church-at-large.  The original translation of this letter is lost; only a Latin one remains.  However, this latter translation is rejected by most historians as "bristling with difficulties" and portrays accurately the immense problems of forged and doctored manuscripts from the earliest days of the Church, falsified documents meant to enhance the position of a power-seeking hierarchy and its retinue.  The disputed passage of the "Latin translation" offered by the Roman archivists as "authentic", which it is not, says:

"But it would be very tedious to enumerate the succession of all the Churches.  We will trace that of the very great and most ancient Church... which was founded and established at Rome by the two very glorious apostles Paul and Peter:  which possesses a tradition which comes from the apostles as much as the faith declared unto men, and which has transmitted it to us through the succession of her bishops: by what we confound all those who in any manner whatsoever, either through blindness or bad intention, do not gather where they should; for every Church, that is to say, the faithful, who are from all placed obliged to go toward that Church, because of the most powerful principality.  In this Church the tradition of the apostles has been preserved by those who are of all countries." *(Ad Hæreses, Lib. III, Cap. iii)*

**This** is indeed a very deficient translation of the original Greek, and obviously has been heavily edited. However, from what we know of later, more famous, forgeries of this type, it is not surprising, nor unusual. The author of this edited version seems to be saying that men must look to Rome for guidance in all things. However, Irenæus was speaking of those who had fled other Churches because of heresy and who now were in the "region of the Romans." The most important Church in that place was, of course, Rome, and he thought it necessary to advise those who were in need of protection to seek the apostolic see nearest them. Irenæus was too good an historian to make blunders as serious as those which appear in this redacted, self-serving testimony.

Let us look carefully at this revised letter and investigate the "difficulties" with the translation, and why historians reject it as a spurious document, edited for selfish reasons and contentious demands.

First, the Roman Church is not "THE MOST ANCIENT CHURCH." Similar Christian communities, in other places, were founded much before that at Rome. If we are to believe either Paul or Peter established the Church at Rome, which they did not, then we must also admit that they could only have done so about thirty years after the Resurrection. Certainly, we know from Scripture that many Churches were inaugurated years before that of the Imperial City.

Second, the controversies with Anicetus and Victor of Rome, their rescripts to other Churches, and the rejection of papal claims by every Church in Christendom, respectively negate any claim that others were "confounded" by Rome's "powerful principality." Quite clearly, the second edition was composed at a time when Rome was still smarting from the many rebuffs she received at the hands of the Greek and African bishops in her midst while seeking to assert herself by any means possible.

As a result of this forgery (scandalous in fact), no respectable Church historian worth his name will accept the letter as genuine. It was obviously altered to enhance the position of the Roman See! Nonetheless, it is one of the three proofs that Rome offers in defense of her supremacy. Very poor proof at that!

It is a serious indictment of our tendency, indeed need, to believe ingested historical facts without testing, that the faithful accept such a poorly formed document as accurate. Even Roman Catholic theologians and historians are embarrassed by this Latin translation and offer no defense as to its authenticity.

Another early document by St. Cyprian (*On the Unity of the Catholic Church*) also extant in two editions relates to the primacy of the Bishop of

Rome. The first version contains some very flattering remarks regarding the Roman See; however, in the a later edition, composed about 255 these references to "Roman primacy" are omitted. By doing so St. Cyprian, who also bore the title of "Pope" at Carthage, is adamant about his position.

"Cyprian, seeing what the Roman Church was doing to his words of mere flattery, felt obliged to write a second version in which all references to Rome were omitted. He clearly wants to say, 'But I never meant that,' and he seems to go out of his way in the revised edition to down-play any overweening admiration of the Roman See." (Wm. Jurgens, *Faith of the Early Fathers*, Vol. I)

Roman Catholic historian P. Benevot summarizes the matter succinctly, sadly relating this incident in his exhaustive work, *Ancient Christian Writers*, Vol. 25, pp. 7-8:

"Cyprian never held that the Pope possessed universal jurisdiction, but he never had to deny it either; in truth, he never asked himself a question about authority in the Church." *(ibid.)*

Sympathetic Roman writers then annex an explanation that this doctrine was always "implicit" in the Church and being developed, a weak argument at best! Obviously, to Rome, most of the Church at the time of Cyprian had not developed to the point of "truth", since a number of early Christian leaders spent an inordinate amount of effort defending themselves against papal encroachments, pretentious lecturing, and their incipient designs on the struggling faith.

It is intriguing to note that Pope Leo XIII himself omits those very flattering and false words of praise for Rome in his encyclical *On the Unity of the Church* (1896), yet he did not disown them. Historians simply attach no credibility to the forged version of the document as mirroring the true mind of that great Church Father, Cyprian of Carthage:

"None of us may set himself up as bishop of bishops, nor compel his brothers to obey him; every bishop of the Church has full liberty and complete power: as he cannot be judged by another, neither can he judge another." (*Council Carth. Cyprian*, pp. 329-330, Benedictine Edition)

Nevertheless, despite Roman claims of developing doctrine, the entire incident takes on a new emphasis when we read Cyprian's words, written a few months later, in which he finds it possible to refer to the words of the reigning Pope Stephen I of Rome as "arrogant, extraneous, and self-contradictory." *(Letter 74)*

From the commentary *Twentieth Century Watch: Apostolic Authority* comes the remarkably insightful observation:

"Though the Roman Catholic Church claims the Fathers as one of their authorities, they seem to reject the pronouncements of these same Fathers, accepting only selectively from their writings, as they desire."

Cyprian was not opposed to a hierarchy; he opposed an "exclusive eldership," and of course he is quoted *selectively* in Roman publications. Regardless, there are respected Roman scholars who admit that he was very much against the idea of an imperial hierarchy. In the introductory notes on Cyprian's writings by Roberts and Donaldson we record the following:

"It (Cyprian's writing) embodies no hierarchical assumption, no 'lordship over God's heritage', but is conceived in the spirit of (St.) Peter when he disclaimed all this and said: 'the presbyters who are among you I exhort, I who am also a presbyter...' (I Peter 5:1) Nothing can be more delusive than the idea that the medieval system (of Roman Catholic government) derives any support from Cyprian's theory of the episcopate or of subsequent Church organization. His was the system of universal parity and community of bishops. In Cyprian's scheme, the apostolate was perpetuated in the episcopate." *(Ante-Nicene Fathers, Vol. V, p. 263)*

Further study of Cyprian's words extracts additional thoughts on the primacy:

"For neither did Peter, whom first the Lord chose... when Paul disputed with him afterwards about the circumcision, claim anything to himself insolently, nor arrogantly assume anything, SO AS TO SAY THAT HE HELD THE PRIMACY, and that he ought to be obeyed by novices and those lately come." *(Ante-Nicene Fathers, Vol. V, p. 377)*

Cyprian did not believe for one instant that Peter, let alone future Bishops of Rome, held any primacy of jurisdiction over the universal Church. In modest terms we are forced to admit that neither did Peter insist on his "rights" when confronted by Paul, which he surely would have done had he held primatial jurisdiction! (Galatians 2:11) On issues so grave for the future and growth of the Church no one bishop today may insist on supreme jurisdiction since there is no precedent either in Holy Scripture or history for such usurpation of exclusive leadership in the Church.

Raymond E. Brown, a well-known Roman Catholic theologian, in *Priest and Bishop: Biblical Reflections,* while specifically discussing the matter of Peter as Bishop of Rome and the subsequent rush to claim control of the universal Church, comments:

"An ancient tradition reports that Peter was the first Bishop of Rome. This seems quite unlikely from what we now know of Christianity at Rome."

Brown goes on to say it is his judgement that even though the possibility of Peter ever being a bishop of Rome is doubtful, it does not necessarily "weaken" the primacy of the papacy. Regardless, he does not expand on just what that "primacy" entails, although Fr. Brown is too good a scholar to confuse primacy of honor with the ersatz doctrine of infallibility.

Fr. Brown also quotes D. W. O'Connor in what he judges to be the "latest, detailed work on the subject of Peter in Rome",

"That Peter founded the Church at Rome is extremely doubtful, and that he served as its first bishop for even one year, much less the twenty-five year period that the (Roman Church) claimed for him, is an unfounded tradition that can be traced back to a point no earlier than the third century. ...furthermore there is no mention of the Roman episcopacy of Peter in the New Testament, I Clement, or the Epistles of Ignatius. ... By the third century, however, the early assumptions based upon intervention (by the Roman Church) or vague, unfounded tradition, have been transformed into 'facts' of history." (D. W. O'Connor, *Peter in Rome*, p. 207)

Regardless of contemporary views, one does not have to depend solely on modern historical research for a picture of Roman "primacy". During the Council of Carthage in 256, Cyprian together with eighty-seven other bishops heartily condemned Stephen, Pope of Rome, for setting himself up as "Bishop of Bishops" and using "tyrannical terror to coerce his colleagues into the necessity of obeying." *(Letter 73)*

Another vocal bishop, Firmillian, informed Cyprian that the Roman bishop's pretensions to "observe ancient customs is false" since "they do not do everything exactly as is done at Jerusalem." Cyprian summed up the feelings of the early Church in relation to the role of bishops, proclaiming for all the world to hear:

**"In the administration of the Church each bishop has the free discretion of his own will, having to account only to the Lord for his actions."**
— *Council Carth. Cyprian,* Benedictine Edition

To illustrate that the early Church did indeed accept St. Cyprian's view of an independent episcopate, it is necessary to relate the incident of Basilides and Martialis, bishops of Spain, charged with apostasy. The accused bishops approached Stephen of Rome for judgement, he being their Metropolitan. Pope Stephen accepted the case and reinstated the errant bishops to their sees. To gain additional support for their cause, the hierarchs sought the corroboration of Cyprian, who was a luminary of the

Church at that time and whose assistance would be valuable in their appeal. Cyprian defended the principle that "other apostles were the same as Peter, endowed with an equal partnership of HONOR AND POWER ...a 'college' *(co-sacerdotes)."* In agreeing to accept the hearing, Cyprian summoned a council of thirty-seven bishops to decide the issue in autumn 254. The initial recommendation of Pope Stephen was overturned, and the Cyprianic council declared the bishops apostates — informing their congregations in Spain to reject them as errant and "undeserving" of episcopal office, which they did. (Account from Frend, *The Rise of Christianity*, pp. 353-354, *summarized*)

In a work dealing with the papal claims in the Patristic era, J. McCue, a historian/theologian, comments on his research:

"In neither case (i.e., Victor or Stephen) can it be shown that Rome was acting out a theory of its own primacy, and in both cases the evidence indicates that the others involved did not suppose that Rome had the authority over other bishops and Churches."

Early Church history "presupposes a regional leadership of Rome, but indicates nothing more. Thus, one concludes that down through the Council of Nicæa, a Roman universal primacy of jurisdiction exists neither as a theoretical construction nor as a *de facto* practice awaiting theoretical interpretation." (J. McCue, "Roman Primacy in the Patristic Era", in P. Empie & T. Murphy, eds., *Papal Primacy*, p. 72)

Examples such as these clearly show that from the beginning of Christian history the early Church was shocked and dismayed, yet unafraid to vigorously condemn the Bishops of Rome when they demanded that other Churches blindly obey their commands. This fact alone is certain proof that no such thing as "universal jurisdiction", let alone "infallibility", existed or was tolerated in the emerging Church. There is simply no doubt in the minds of serious historians that the "primacy" granted the Church at Rome was merely a respectful admission that the bishops of that Church were "first among equals" — a position secured by that city's noble place in the secular world. There existed no office of jurisdiction which the later papacy demanded and, through deceit, attempted to secure. The fact that Rome was *a seat* of the origin and life of the episcopacy was never disputed, and the early Church knew that it must maintain unity with Rome even though its bishops waxed arrogant and insisted on insufferable obedience, a position EVERY Church found intolerable at best!

Both John Meyendorff and W. De Vries, historians of the Eastern Church, are compelled to admit that "the attitude of the Oriental Church with regard to Rome does not recognize any authority which is simultaneously juridical and universal. Even the right of a juridical appeal to Rome is nowhere acknowledged at this time." (Bermejo, *Towards Christian Reunion,* p. 113)

Furthermore, scholars conversant with the history of the early Church, De Vries, J.D. Mansi and others, see the so-called "primacy of Rome" as severely restricted and not at all in tandem with that all-inclusive jurisdiction claimed by the papacy.

Shortly after the incident of Cyprian vs. Stephen the aforementioned Firmillian of Cappodocia sternly warned Pope Stephen that if, by his arrogance, he attempted to excommunicate anyone disagreeing with the Roman Church, he would accomplish only "excommunication of yourself from all." "You are blind in error," Firmillian warned Stephen, and as a result he was to be ignored. Firmillian was unyielding in his assertion that Stephen's ideas of a Roman bishop's pretensions and universal jurisdiction were totally "fallacious; 'Qualis vero error sit et quanta cæcitas eius.'" ["As great as the error is, even greater is his blindness."] *(Letter LXXV, par. 16)*

Simmering resentment soon flared into open conflict. In A.D. 340, Pope Julius of Rome admitted into his communion several members of the hierarchy who had been excommunicated by the Eastern Church. Bishops of that Church were shocked beyond belief; nevertheless, their response was swift and unambiguous. They reiterated that the Church did not center at Rome, but allowed for a larger entity than merely "one bishop, one rule". At the Second Council of Constantinople, held in 381, the cry rose from the assembled bishops, "Christ came to us from the East," and soon the bishops of Gaul and England, chafing from Roman pretensions, took up the cause. St. Columbanus (c. 540-615), in hostile (and most unyielding) letters addressed to the Roman Pope, showed the Irish Church to be unconcerned with the papacy — a distant thing not really affecting its life! Later in the twelfth century the English Church via the celebrated *York Tracts* echoed the same concerns, and Avitus, Gallic Bishop of Vienne, addressed the Patriarch of Jerusalem:

"Your Church exercises the primacy and has 'principem locum' (principal place) in the Church." *(Works of P. Sirmond Avitus, vol. 2)*

The right to appeal to Rome was originally limited to the so-called Suburbicarian Provinces in central and southern Italy and the adjacent islands offshore. The Bishop of Rome could judge only cases within this area. However, about 370 this right was extended to most of the inhabited Western Empire first by Valentinian I, and then by his son Gratian. Ultimately, through the influence of Pope Leo, the right to judge was extended by Valentinian II in 445. Leo also claimed the right as belonging to him because he was the successor of Peter. This claim was more fully developed by Gregory (the Great) who was assisted by the conditions of his era. However, the pope's jurisdiction did not extend to the Celtic Churches, those in the north, those outside the Empire, and the entire Eastern Church.

In summarizing the facts of ecclesiastical leadership during this very important developmental stage of the Church's life, we again turn to W. H. C. Frend:

"At the same time, acceptance of Rome as a 'leading see' *(principalis)* implied no jurisdictional rights for its bishop. If Stephen could be expected to discipline Marcian of Arles for his lapse into Novatianism, he could equally stand rebuked by Cyprian's council summoned to hear the complaints of the Spanish congregations against his decision to restore lapsed bishops to their sees. Stephen and his Church could also be in error, appealing to 'human tradition, not legitimate' and persisting in their mistaken views. In the minds of many North African Christians, Peter and Paul were 'pillars of discipline', 'spiritual men', 'martyrs', with whom the suffering North African Church could be associated. Their episcopal successors had no particular claim to obedience. Nonetheless, the Roman Church was coming to be considered in the *West* as a pivot of episcopal government.

"In the East, while some bishops were simply embarrassed by Stephen's claims, others were as forthright in their denunciation of them as the North Africans. For Firmillian, Stephen could be 'blind and in error,' a prey to wrongheaded custom and on the way to excommunicating himself. Ideas based on his succession to Peter were fallacious. In calmer moods, however, the Petrine texts were interpreted allegorically, leading to a more general sense being attributed to them than in the West. They were referred by Origen and his successors to 'the Church', or 'the faithful,' and not to Peter himself. Commenting on Matt. 16:18, Origen stated that 'the Rock' was 'every imitator of Christ from whom they drank, who drank from the spiritual Rock that followed them.' The Church and its constitution were built on such a Rock. The passage referred to the apostles as a whole and not only to Peter. Elsewhere, Peter is seen as the pattern of all who had a right disposition for building the Church. The 'keys of the kingdom' were given to all who believed in the confession Peter made and repented their faults. Origen's lead was followed. In the fifth century, we find the Alexandrian Monophysite patriarch, Timothy Aelurus (454-77), writing to the Church of Constantinople and referring to Peter's Rock as 'meaning the orthodox faith', and not Peter's successors.

"For some Easterns, including the historian Eusebius, James rather than

Peter was preeminent as a bishop, as 'brother of Christ,' who received the episcopate at Jerusalem 'from the Savior and the apostles.' Respect for the Roman see, as Origen shows (Eusebius, *HE*, VI.14.10), was connected with its antiquity and perhaps also with the primacy of the city of Rome as capital of the Empire. (W.H.C. Frend, *The Rise of Christianity*, pp. 400-401)

While the Church struggled to maintain itself in a hostile environment internal disputes weakened its witness to an unbelieving world. The observation of a pagan historian, Ammianus Marcellinus (4th century) has been handed down through the centuries: "No wild beasts are as hostile to humans as Christians are to one another." This certainly weakened the basic Christian message of brotherhood and solidarity. Christian churchmen, too, were dismayed by Rome's tactics. Frend observes:

"In 382, Pope Damasus of Rome boldly proclaimed that the unique authority of the Council of Nicæa rested on the fact that its decisions were "ratified" by his predecessor Sylvester I of Rome, a boast completely without foundation. However, we must keep in mind that this was the same Damasus who coined the term "Apostolic See" in sole reference to the Roman Church, and about whom St. Basil of Cæsarea spoke bitterly, "a man so exaltedly removed from the earth and enthroned so high that the voices which speak the truth from below are unable to get through to him."

Damasus asserted that the Church in Egypt was founded by St. Mark in the name of the Roman Pope — a claim the Egyptian Church found ridiculous. Later, he insisted that all decisions of Church councils be ratified by the Bishop of Rome, a demand not only without precedent in Church history, but embarrassing for a community struggling to maintain itself in a hostile and difficult epoch. A vast number of the episcopate ignored Damasus' demands, and in a pique he called his own council to proclaim Roman superiority. Of course, his pronouncements were again ignored and this reigning Pope lost all credibility with disbelieving bishops throughout most of the Catholic Church.

St. Basil of Cæsaræa complains bitterly, in two private letters to friends, of the "haughtiness, despotic arrogance and cold indifference" of Damasus (Epistles 215 and 239). Historian Amand de Mendieta in his study of St. Basil, writing in *Biblical and Patristic Studies* (1963, pp. 122-166), characterizes the Bishop of Cæsarea's writings as void of any proof "that he took seriously the Roman ideology…of the primacy by divine right and of the jurisdiction of the Bishop of Rome… Basil has never explicitly repudiated this primacy; he has simply ignored it."

Pope Damasus weathered many controversies, but was finally brought to trial by a Synod of his own bishops in 378 and ultimately forced to defend himself against a number of very serious charges. Among them was murder, for his part in the October 26th (366 A.D.) massacre of 137 people on Rome's Esquiline Hill, the result of the bitter feud which preceded appointment of a bishop for Rome. Because of Damasus' friendship with the Emperor Gratian and the support of numerous Roman *matronae* (wealthy women), he was exonerated; however, several scathing indictments exist on record by contemporaries, i.e., Ammianus, Valentinian, and others who saw in this pope a "pretentious, notorious and vain 'ear-tickler." *(Collectio Avellana, 1:10, p. 4)*

Damasus is almost unknown to contemporary laymen, a footnote in history, since he was far surpassed in character and ability by St. Basil in the East and St. Ambrose of Milan, who was called the "true pope" of the Western Church by churchmen of his time.

With the onset of the reign of St. Constantine (313 A.D.), Christianity was transformed from a persecuted religion to a privileged faith. When the emperor moved the capital of the empire to Constantinople, the patriarch of that city was thrust into a unique position of leadership, unchallenged by the Bishop of Rome. The latter's previous position within the Church was eclipsed, although most Roman popes remained steadfast in the faith even through its darkest moments.

During this time of lessened influence for the Church at Rome, its fortunes were tied closely to the vagaries of the secular state. Until the year 741, all papal elections had to be confirmed by the emperor at Ravenna, Italy. Clearly, the Western Church needed a visible leader during this period to combat the growing influence of hostile forces intent on dissolving its role in society. Therefore the emperor gave the Roman Church certain limited jurisdiction to bolster its own position and to mediate any disputes which might threaten the unity of the Western portion of the Empire. However, as we have seen, the Churches in Britain, Ireland, and Milan, along with certain bishops in Gaul unaffected by such decrees, retained complete autonomy and sovereignty afforded by centuries of tradition and practice.

For those who might be tempted to exalt the position of the Bishop of Rome and see in the independence of various local Churches a spirit of revolt—it is useful to quote the epitome of *Canon 6 of the First Ecumenical Council of Nicæa* (325 A.D.), which states:

**"The Bishop of Alexandria shall have complete control and jurisdiction over Egypt, Libya and the Pentapolis. As also the Roman bishop over those as are subject to Rome. So too, the Bishop of Antioch and the rest of the bishops shall have complete control and jurisdiction over those faithful who are under them."**

Episcopal leaders were saying, in effect: "Rome, we accept your honorable status in the Church; however, you go too far with your presumptions."

Some revisionist historians, Orthodox, Roman and Reformed, seem to "unduly weaken" the meaning of the various conciliar canons on jurisdiction. Luis Bermejo castigates their timidness by boldly asserting the authentic meaning of jurisdiction in the early Church, which is summarized in the following passage:

The Council of "Nicæa (325) looks up to Rome as a prestigious See of apostolic origin…but ecclesiologically, according to this Council, Alexandria, Antioch and Rome are on an equal level, each endowed with the SAME power within its provincial boundaries."

However, Rome could not stop there. It began to usurp an unusual amount of authority, and in a letter to the universal Church composed at the famous rump Council of Sardica (343 A.D.) Rome claimed universal jurisdiction over all of Christendom. Therefore eighty Eastern bishops, in response to this unheard of call to total control over the Church, refused to accept that Oriental (Eastern) bishops should be judged or ordered by Rome. In addition, they were outraged to learn that bishops expelled from the Church by a lawful Eastern synod were reinstated by Rome, which acted alone and with no authority to make such a unilateral decision.

As a result of these conflicts, we read in the highly informative and very authoritative ancient documents *Collectanea Antiariana Parisina (A, IV)* the following condemnation of Rome's self-imposed and fictional authority over the Church at large. The majority bishops, seeing Rome's desire for hegemony, wrote:

**(We protest strongly)… "the novelty, which is abhorrent to the ancient custom of the Church, that that which has been decided by an Oriental Council of bishops should be revoked by a Western bishop." At the conclusion of the documents Pope Julius is censured with an anathema.**

During those dark days for the Church at Rome, bishops of that city were often ordered to change or amend doctrine and wink at tradition, or face the awesome power of the secular government.  For example, Pope John I was enjoined by the Emperor Theodoric, King of Italy, to travel to Constantinople to plead with the emperor on behalf of the Arians (a heretical sect).  When John failed in his mission, he was imprisoned, and from this period onwards the popes of Rome experienced a definite emasculation in regard to their influence, lasting for several hundred years.

Meanwhile, the Church in the East continued to go its own way. Subsequent to events in the West, the universal Council of Chalcedon (451) gave Constantinople equal rank in honor with Rome.  Needless to say, by this behavior the Church was now doing the very thing Christ so clearly forbade:

"An argument broke out among the disciples, as to who was to be the greatest.  Jesus said, but this is not the way it is with you" (Luke 22:24-27).

In essence, the world was treated to the spectacle of Church leaders spouting words of competition and condemnation as to who was the greatest and most honorable among them, while discounting the teaching that Christ's leaders were to be true servants, not masters, of the flock! Nevertheless, men vied for power and prestige and Leo of Rome became enraged when he felt that the influence of Constantinople, a See of which he was already jealous, was unfairly heightened.  Leo complained strenuously, but his objections were in vain.  Verified by the decisions of Chalcedon (680; Canon 28:36), Constantinople, now called "New Rome," began to assume the rights and prerogatives of "Old Rome". Constantinople's patriarchs were styled "Ecumenical"; consequently, in 595, Pope Gregory of Rome wrote John of Constantinople, since he was clearly worried about the continuing influence of the Eastern Church.  St. Gregory termed John's use of the title "Supreme Bishop of the Universal Church" blasphemous and "against the Gospel of Christ," and wrote the following historic letter, now almost 1400 years old. *(Editor's note: "Supreme Bishop of the Universal Church, a title named "blasphemous" by Pope Gregory, is now one of the official titles of the Roman Pope.)*

"To John, Bishop of Constantinople:

"Your Holiness:

"When the Apostle Paul heard certain of the faithful say: "I am of Paul, or I am of Apollos, or I am of Peter," he could not see them without horror thus dividing the Body of Christ to attach its members to various heads. Paul exclaimed: Was Paul crucified for you? Or were you baptized in the name of Paul?  If he could not bear that the members of the Body of the Lord should be attached piecemeal to other heads than that of Christ, though those heads were apostles, what will you say to Christ Who is head of the universal Church, you, who with your title of universal bishop would bring all the Church members into subjection to yourself?...

"What are your brethren, the bishops of the universal Church, but the stars of God?...

"You know it, my dear brother:  hath not the venerable Council of Chalcedon conferred an honorable title upon the Roman see?  Wherefore I am, by God's will, the servant?  And yet none of us has permitted this title to be given to himself; none has assumed this bold title, lest by assuming a special distinction in the episcopate we should seem to refuse it to all our brethren, our brother bishops."

Your brother, Gregory

What Pope Gregory is saying is clear.  All ecclesiastical authority resides in the office of bishop as a successor of St. Peter, and not in one particular man.  However high on the ecclesiastical ladder one goes the title "universal bishop" is contrary to God's will and word while being, as Gregory himself states, both "vainglorious and wicked."  St. Gregory concludes only what can be concluded, that no bishop may claim sovereignty over another bishop without invading the rights and prerogatives of the entire episcopal college.  St. Gregory, Bishop of Rome, who raised the status of the Western Church to amazing heights, proclaims the fatal words himself regarding the office of "universal bishop":

"Peter was given the keys to the celestial kingdom.  The power to bind and loose was given to him.  The care of the Church and the primacy were committed to him; and yet Peter could not call himself the universal apostle. But the Bishop John, my brother in the priesthood, would fain assume the title of Bishop of the Universal Church.  I can only exclaim, O tempora! O mores!"

"Who, against the precepts of the Gospel and the decrees of the canons, has the presumption to usurp a new title?  Would to heaven that there be only one.  Who, wishing to lessen the other bishops, desired to be called Universal Bishop of the Church?"

"If any one usurp in the Church a title which embraces all the faithful, the universal Church — O blasphemy! — will then fall with him, since he makes himself to be called universal.  **May all Christians reject this blasphemous title — the title which takes the sacerdotal honor from every priest the moment it is insanely usurped by one bishop!"** *(Letters of St. Gregory, Book V, Letter 20)*

**Note:** The full title of the Pope, the Bishop of Rome, in use since the First Vatican Council in 1870, contains these words:

"His Holiness the Pope, Bishop of Rome and Vicar of Jesus Christ, Successor of St. Peter, Prince of the Apostles, *Supreme Pontiff (Bishop) of the Universal Church*, Patriarch of the West, Primate of Italy, Archbishop and Metropolitan of the Roman Province, Sovereign of Vatican City." (Taken directly from the *Official Catholic Directory*, J.P. Kenedy and Sons, NY)

Therefore, according to one of the greatest popes of the Roman Church, Christians should reject one who assumes the "blasphemous" title "Bishop of the Universal Church," for it is an "imitation of the devil." In his famous speech to Vatican Council I, Bishop Joseph George Strossmayer of Bosnia notes that Pope Gregory titled any hierarch who assumes the name "Universal Bishop" an "Antichrist". (Strossmayer: 1870, Florence Ver.; given in full later in this work)

---

## THE MYTH OF "INFALLIBILITY" EMERGES

Aside from the obvious difficulties with an all-encompassing primacy accorded to the Roman bishop, there is a dogma (quite simply a teaching of the Church which must be believed in order to be saved) professed by Rome which strains one's imagination to the breaking-point. That is the dogma of infallibility!

Until the thirteenth century there was never a shred of evidence, either in history or Scripture, as to the so-called "infallibility" of the Bishop of Rome. Actually, it was not until centuries later that the specific term "infallible" would be used — and then only in reference to a succession of truths within the Christian faith. These truths could not be changed; they were irreformable — therefore permanent, infallible and unyielding. Modestly stated, in what could be called the infancy of "infallibility", the term clearly did not apply to an office, nor a man, but to the unfailing, orthodox faith of the apostles.

Interestingly enough it was the eccentric Franciscan monk Peter Olivi, who in the thirteenth century claimed a "special gift" for the papal office, although Olivi was much more interested in the political ramifications of such a theory than in any doctrinal implications. Practical application of this theory began when Nicholas II, pope from 1277-80, pronounced that Franciscan poverty was a noble ideal and quite worthy of emulation by the clergy and faithful alike. Olivi, a staunch proponent of the evangelical counsel, claimed that as a result of this papal edict, teachings of pontiffs were "irreversible". Nevertheless, some forty years after Nicholas' death, Pope John XXII came to a much different conclusion about the issue of vowed poverty. When various Franciscans appealed to the "binding decision" of Nicholas, Pope John rejected this "infallibility mentality" as an encroachment upon his rights as pope. In the Bull *"Qui Quorundum"* *(1324)*, John condemned the "doctrine" of unchangeable papal decrees as the "work of Satan." Papal historians gloss over this incident as an embarrassment — and well it is! Interestingly enough, Pope John was later to retract other past papal teachings as false — including one teaching regarding the Beatific Vision — on his deathbed!

Brian Tierney in his now-definitive research into the origins of papal infallibility goes farther and notes that the words "pernicious audacity" and "pestiferous doctrine" were applied by *"Qui Quorundum"* to Olivi's claims of this "special gift" of popes which only later came to be named "infallibility".

To understand the genesis and development of the doctrine of infallibility, its checkered past, its acceptance, repudiation, re-acceptance and ultimate enthronement, one must, of course, start at the beginning, exploring the teaching of the papal office from Rome's position as an honorable see within the early Church, to her role as a political pawn in the medieval period of ecclesiastical intrigue. In doing this, we must recognize that, for the better part of this work, we have been discussing the position of the Bishop of Rome within the Church from the apostolic age; therefore, we know that these bishops were honored for their learning, yet frequently chastised for their increasing arrogance, by more humble Church leaders. We know also that Rome often came down squarely on the side of orthodoxy during disputes which raged around the infant faith. Nevertheless, it is an indisputable fact that several popes at Rome were officially condemned for their heretical views and denial of apostolic faith, teaching and tradition. Of course, these condemnations preclude any defense of "infallibility" for a number of technical reasons, but also for the very logical determination that if one, or more, popes taught heresy in the past, what is to prevent a present or future pope from doing the same?

Luis Bermejo summarizes the preceding history into a concise, yet cogent, prelude to the events at Vatican Council I:

"For now we know that the novel doctrine of papal infallibility was proposed for the first time around 1280 by Olivi, an eccentric Franciscan who, in the midst of the controversy on poverty, sought by means of the new theory not to extol but to restrict pontifical power, since, on the basis of his opinion, each pope would be bound by the "infallible" definitions of his predecessors. Pope John XXII, who clearly perceived the unacceptable limitations Olivi's theory would impose on his power, rejected it as a 'pestiferous doctrine', a 'pernicious audacity'. The 12th century canonists taught both the indefectibility of the Church and the position of the Roman See as a court of appeal, but they failed to draw the doctrine of papal infallibility from either of these two premises. In the course of Vatican I (some) argued *ex silentio:* the early centuries certainly knew of, but did not explicitly state, their belief in papal infallibility. In reality this opinion was totally unknown before 1280; then it erupted suddenly under suspicious circumstances — only to be quickly condemned by John XXII. By the beginning of the 19th century the theory of papal infallibility had been rejected almost everywhere (with the exception of the Roman school). Hence, at Vatican I we are faced with the rather disturbing phenomenon of a doctrine which is catapulted from rejection to dogma in the comparatively short span of 70 years." *(Towards Christian Reunion)*

Popes were condemned by the universal Church as early as 295 A.D.; however, grave difficulties for Roman bishops originated in 417 with Pope Zosimus who foolishly reversed his predecessor's condemnation of an early heretic named Pelagius. Under extreme pressure from the African Church, coupled with an explicit threat of losing his power base in the papal election of 419, Zosimus reversed himself again and anathematized this Breton monk after whom the heresy (Pelagianism) was named. Thus we become witnesses to a pained scenario of a pope supporting a declared heretic, relenting, then condemning him under coercion from other patriarchs (most anxious to prevent one of their own from becoming marked as a heretic), while claiming a teaching authority even he was unable to discern.

An intriguing sidelight to the sad tale of Zosimus is that he later tried to assert his "authority" within the African Church; however, he was soundly rebuffed by revered leaders of the Church assembled there in council. Zosimus' successor, Boniface I, obviously smarting from the rebuff to papal pretensions, attempted precisely the same action in 419. He was again roundly condemned by nearly two hundred bishops gathered in Alexandria. In 426, Pope Cælestinus of Rome renewed this continuing struggle to assume control of the African Church, but was tersely warned against sending even a low-level delegate from Rome to Africa. A document of censure was subsequently circulated by these local bishops decrying the Roman belief that God would confer "universal" authority and judgement upon a "foreign" bishop (i.e., Roman pope), while denying it to a large and prayerful assembly of obviously sincere churchmen gathered to deliberate within their own country. This last futile attempt by Rome effectively ended papal interference in the affairs of the African Church, a Church which proved a most inexorable nemesis to the pretensions of Roman bishops, and which remained a bulwark against heresy and ecclesiastical corruption during the most formidable period of the infant Church.

A further case in point concerned Pope Vigilius (537-555), who was summarily ordered to Constantinople, bitter rival of Rome, in 548, where he signed the condemnation of Theodore of Mopsuestia (and others) accused of heresy. After bitter opposition, Vigilius withdrew his signature from the document. A Council of bishops was convoked in Constantinople (553) which strongly censured Theodore's group and its writings (i.e., *The Three Chapters*). Again, after several changes of mind the vacillating Pope Vigilius assented to the council's demands and headed home for Rome. He was violently condemned by the Church there and was replaced by the deacon Pelagius, who was championed by the emperor. Vigilius was eventually forced to subscribe to the council's decisions and castigated for his initial support of heresy, while a number of local Churches formally excommunicated him from their midst. Vigilius died in prison before reaching the capital city.

Bermejo's summary and verdict in the affair of Pope Vigilius vs. council are concise. "In the Acts of the Council of Constantinople II we read, 'In matters of faith no one can prejudge a question for the universal faith, for we all need the help of one another.' This was an obvious reference to Vigilius. The Emperor then goes on to declare that Pope Vigilius has cut himself off from the Church Catholic by his defense of the impiety contained in *(the Chapters)* and by doing so he has 'cut himself off from our communion.' (ACO IV/1, 209) The council concurred and the pope's name was stricken from the diptychs.

"Six months after the council closed the pope bowed to its wishes and repudiated the so-called *'Three Chapters'*, a heretical document. Sharply differing conceptions of authority, papal and conciliar, had come to a head and clashed, and it was the latter that prevailed, forcing Rome to retract its stand and back down." (*Toward Christian Reunion*, 122)

Once again we turn to the towering and scholarly tome by W. H. C. Frend, *The Rise of Christianity*, recently published, containing the results of exciting contemporary research along with the findings of thirty-one "new" letters of St. Augustine (Johannes Divjak, editor). This research proclaims unequivocally that:

"Fortunately for the North African (Church), such cases where the appellate jurisdiction of the papacy was tested were thoroughly discreditable to the appellants... *Letter IX* and *Letter XX* show that appeals to Rome on disciplinary matters affecting bishops were not uncommon, but that the role of the papacy was usually confined to *upholding* the decisions of the North African disciplinary tribunals. The North Africans were prepared to invoke conciliar canons... (and) the importance of conciliar authority becomes clear (by their doing so)..." *(Letters of Augustine: Johannes Divjak, ed.)* A practical case in point follows.

"A priest named Apiarius... committed serious offenses and was deposed by his bishop, Urbanus. (Apiarius) took his case to Rome" (the nearest apostolic See). "...Once again the North African conciliar system proved too strong for the papacy. (The North Africans) assembled (their) council. On May 1, 418, at the same time it unanimously condemned Pelagius, the council forbade 'presbyters, deacons and inferior clergy' to appeal overseas" (i.e., Rome, or other places). (Canon 17) (W.H.C. Frend, *op.cit.*)

But the upshot was that the North African Church council exposed the fraudulent, and quite untrue, statements of Rome claiming its authority to hear appeals from lower clergy and bishops of any Church when first recourse failed. Rome insisted that the famed Nicene Council gave it appeal rights. This was a bold-faced lie. The only "authority" given to Rome was given to itself through its local rump Council of Sardica — a far less authoritative council than Nicæa. Thus, with this action, the African Church outwitted the papacy and effectively stopped Roman interference for once and for all.

These few examples clearly show that in the sixth century the Bishop of Rome was regarded neither as infallible nor as the "center" of Catholic unity. The actual center of unity was firmly believed to reside in the pure and unchanging faith of the apostles and the councils of the Church, which defined and interpreted that faith. Accordingly, the center of the Church was seen to reside in Holy Scripture as witnessed to, and enumerated in, the creeds. Only the Word of God made manifest in such a manner obliged believers, if they expected to be numbered among the faithful members of Christ's Church.

**Note:** Other pertinent examples of autonomy on the part of "local Churches" show that in the Metropolitan of Milan severed communion with the Church at Rome for 18 years, and the Church in Aquileia went its own way for 147 years.  Others who did likewise were the Celtic Church, of course the aforementioned African Church, and the entire Eastern Church focused in Jerusalem and Constantinople.  Obviously, the Catholic Church was not a monolithic body powered by its heart at Rome, but a Church bound by the Sacred Scriptures and the ancient creeds, with a foundation embracing a personal faith in Christ Jesus.  One interesting adjunct to the independence shown by various Churches is a letter written by St. Columban of Ireland early in the seventh century reminding the Pope at Rome that although he was bishop of an ancient See, nevertheless he should "yield the primacy to Jerusalem." *(Jerusalem and Rome: Chadwick and von Campenhausen, p. 31)*

*"This people honors me with their lips.  But their heart is very far from me. …in vain do they worship me, teaching as doctrines the precepts of men."  (Mark 7:7)*

In perspective, however, even these situations pale when contrasted with the far more notorious incident of Honorius, Pope of Rome from 625-638 A.D.  A very abbreviated scenario would read something like this.  The great controversy of the seventh century was whether Christ had one or two wills — not a minor theological point, although quite technical to some degree.  The Monothelite doctrine ascribed a single will to the incarnate Christ.  The initial interventions in this controversy by the Bishops of Rome were a complete and devastating fiasco.  Pope Honorius in 638 wrote to Constantinople proclaiming his support for the one-will doctrine, and condemned anyone who accepted the two-will formula.  The Third Council of Constantinople (680-681) repudiated the one-will formula, naming supporters of it "anathema" — and thus Honorius stood condemned as a heretic, a judgement repeated by the Second Council of Nicæa in 787, and the Fourth Council of Constantinople in 869-870.  Up to the eleventh century, every Bishop of Rome was required to reaffirm the decision of the Sixth Council (i.e., its condemnation of Honorius) before assuming the papal office.  The crucial matter here was not the difficulty with doctrine, which was basically a matter of language, but the fact that the patriarch of the West, the pope, was condemned by a Church council, which was unafraid to confront him and subsequently sever all relationship with one they saw as a notorious heretic!

The Third Council of Constantinople condemned Pope Honorius for heresy; however, the reigning Pope of Rome, Agatho, requested that the council condemn past patriarchs of the Eastern Church for holding views in conflict with the Church at large. The council obliged but in addition on its own authority, and going far beyond the pope's request, included the name of Honorius, whose second letter to Patriarch Sergius was considered heretical. The council declared, "We state that Honorius, once pope of ancient Rome, should be anathematized and expelled from the one, holy, catholic Church of God." (Mansi 11, 555c) The council fathers declared unanimously "So we all believe, there is but one faith, we all concur, we all agree, we all hold the orthodox faith." (Mansi 11, 655)

Other notorious controversies surround popes who were considered "Deprehendatur a Fide Devius" ("caught wandering from the Faith"):

Pope Callistus (221-227) is said by St. Hippolytus, a third century writer, to have been a Unitarian, identifying the Father and the Son as one indivisible Spirit.

Pope Marcellinus (295-304), charged with making sacrifices in public to the pagan gods and surrendering the sacred books to secular authorities;

Pope Liberius (352-366), condemned because he purchased his release from exile by renouncing the Nicene Creed, thus having aided in the condemnation of that great champion of orthodox Christianity, St. Athanasius; and

Pope Anastasius II (496-498), condemned because of his deep friendship and support for those who formulated the Monophysite schism at Constantinople.

(Note: The above examples refer only to doctrinal aberrations, and do not begin to touch upon the subsequent moral wanderings of popes through the centuries of Church history.)

An interesting adjunct to this opportunism on the part of errant popes was the conflict between John XXII (to whom we have already been introduced) and King Philip VI of France. In the fourteenth century Philip ascended the throne and proved to be a devout, yet curious, believer. He was fascinated with the "problem" of the Beatific Vision and whether the souls of the dead see God's face immediately upon entering paradise, or whether they must "linger" until the final judgement day.

This seemingly trivial matter was one of enormous religious and political significance in the Middle Ages. If the blessed ones had to tarry until the day of judgement, then prayers directed to them were effective only if, and when, they were admitted into "God's Holy Presence". The various cults erected around such "saints", their relics and immense revenues, relied solely upon whether the elect could intercede with God for those still living on earth. Philip asked for an opinion from the pope. John replied that there was no Beatific Vision for the recently departed. The King was enraged. Seeing his treasury depleted as the consequence of such a "doctrine", he threatened to burn him (the pope) "like an Albigensian" unless he retracted his opinion. Philip added that if the pope held such views, he would be regarded as a heretic in the Kingdom of France.

A papal commission was hastily convened and "decided" that indeed the souls of the faithful departed experienced the immediate joy of the Beatific Vision. So much for papal pronouncements and Roman expediency!

## The False Documents:  "Forged Proof"

No overview of the papacy would be complete without mention of some very famous documents which for centuries claimed to give complete authority to the Bishop of Rome over all Churches in Christendom. The documents are never mentioned today by the Roman Church, since their origin and content have been proven to be brazen forgeries. Late in the sixteenth century, the *Magdeburg Centuries* exposed these documents as false and totally without historical credence. Therefore, the documents remain an acute repudiation to the papal cause and the theory of infallibility, as well they should!

The first of these documents was fraudulently composed about the middle of the second century, and consisted of several letters and homilies which claimed to have been authored by a certain "Clementine of Rome." They were addressed to "James, Brother of the Lord" and bishop of the first Christian Church — that of Jerusalem. These accounts state that after the death of Peter, St. Clement was appointed as the new Bishop of Rome, at the express wish of Peter himself. In a discourse, St. Peter was made to say, "I impart to Clement the authority of binding and loosing in order that he will decide on earth what will be approved in heaven." This is the only document which Roman theologians can produce as "indisputable evidence" that Peter was the first Bishop of Rome. It was included in every papal pronouncement as a "deed" to the office, yet it is a total fabrication and utterly spurious. Even the most elementary scholarship tells us that there had been two Bishops of Rome before Clement — namely, Linus and Cletus (Anacletus). Therefore those who wished to force the Roman view on the illiterate were induced to explain that Linus and Cletus had been simple bishops and had no need to use the office of Peter, since he was still alive and active. It was only with Peter's death that there was need to explain the fact that Clement became Bishop of Rome about 88 A.D. — over 20 years after the death of St. Peter (A.D. 67). Therefore, Roman apologists have never been able to explain how Peter, dead for 21 years, could nominate Clement as his successor. Needless to say, the documents are now only a historical oddity, and no respected theologian issues them any form of credibility. The power of the papal hierarchy, however, based on fictitious documentation, developed over a number of years. As a result of these forgeries, the wealth and capacity of the Roman Church became very great until, by the mid-eighth century, Stephen III (A.D. 757) secured a signature on a "bequest" by Pepin, King of the Franks, which is referred to as the *Donation of Pepin.* This document supposedly deeded to the Bishop of Rome large areas of northern Italy which were expanded in the late eighth century to include about two thirds of the entire country. Pepin's bequest was attributed to "divine mandate," a desire by God that the papacy be both a spiritual and a temporal power, a theory based on a very faulty interpretation of Luke 22:38. However, because of these forged documents (i.e., the *"Clementine Epistles"* and the *"Donation of Pepin"*) the pope became a secular ruler as well as a spiritual one.

By the mid-ninth century, another series of forged letters, supposedly composed by the Bishops of Rome from St. Clement (A.D. 88) to St. Gregory the Great (A.D. 590), appeared in France under the title *Isidor Mercator.* These letters set down teaching about the complete authority of the Bishops of Rome as clear and acceptable doctrine "directly from Christ's own mouth." The collection of these falsified documents includes "over 100 decrees of 30 popes who occupied the Chair of Peter for the first three centuries." Such forgeries were totally abandoned during the Reformation, when they were found to have been fabricated by those interested solely in a secular kingdom, rather than a spiritual realm.

We may ask why the need arose to manufacture counterfeit documents? One answer might be that the medieval papacy needed to assert its authority in order to combat encroachments by hostile forces outside the Church — some might say within the Church itself. This viewpoint is bolstered by the witness of Hildebrand (Pope Gregory VII, 1073-83), who claimed, "By these documents we aim to show the entire world that we, of our own will, can seize or return kingdoms, principalities, earldoms and entire fortunes of this world, because we the Pope of Rome have the power to bind and unbind". (cf. *Testimonies of the Church*) Of course, few if any written materials could be circulated to combat such invalid claims, or to answer the growing secular power of the papacy, since any book viewed as unfavorable to the papal cause was immediately suppressed by the Roman Church. This meant simply that one writing, distributing, or reading such literature was excommunicated from the Church, and thereby lost any civil rights as well. This effectively limited and controlled powers hostile to the Roman See, and allowed papal polemic to go unchallenged almost to the era of the Reformation.

## AN ISSUE: COUNCILS VS. POPE ALONE

Roman Catholic theologians make two very distinct points when referring to the papacy:

(1) It is an office divinely mandated for the salvation of all men and women.

(2) Nothing is above the pope — he is strictly outside the jurisdiction of any body of bishops (council or synod), or for that matter any person within the secular or religious realm.

Simply stated, no person or assembly can judge, re-order or countermand a papal decree — according to Roman Catholic theology and tradition!

As a consequence, however, one cannot accept this teaching at face value if he understands the function and status of Church councils in history. Reformed theologian Loraine Boettner, in his very informative work *Roman Catholicism,* explains the dilemma history poses for the papal defenders who wish to eliminate the role of deliberative councils in the universal Church.

"The Council of Constance declared that 'every lawfully convoked Ecumenical council representing the Church derives its authority immediately from Christ, and every one, the pope included, is subject to it in matters of faith, in the healing of schism, and the reformation of the Church.' But the Vatican Council of 1870 has decreed that infallibility is vested in the pope alone as head of the Church, when speaking *ex cathedra.*

"There were times during the Middle Ages when the popes increased their power until they were the unquestioned rulers in both the Church and the state. Some deposed kings and lesser civil officials, and could imprison or commit individuals to servitude for life. The decrees of excommunication, directed against individuals, in which those excommunicated were placed outside the protection of the civil law, and the interdict, under which whole nations were branded as outlaws and placed under the ban, were terrible things. Some popes took it upon themselves to declare any political action not pleasing to them null and void, as Innocent III did with Magna Carta after it had been won by the people of England from a despotic king, or as Pius V did in 1570 when he attempted to "uncrown" Queen Elizabeth I of England, and to release the people of England from allegiance to her. The Roman Catholic ideal is that the pope should be able to crown and uncrown kings, and other civil rulers should acknowledge that their power comes from God through the pope as God's representative on earth. Where the Roman Church has been able to realize its ideal, it has made civil rulers vassals of the pope.

"Before 1870 the ultimate authority commonly acknowledged in the Roman Church was the Church speaking through its councils. While the doctrine of papal infallibility had been discussed for some centuries, it had never met with general favor. Instead, it had been repugnant to a large majority of the hierarchy. For nearly two hundred years before the Vatican Council, the Roman Catholic bishops, clergy and laity of England and Ireland had denied that infallibility was a doctrine of the Church. In 1825, for instance, when the restoration of political privileges to English Roman Catholics was under discussion in Parliament, a British government commission asked a panel of Irish Roman Catholics if the Roman Church held that the pope was infallible. The bishops correctly replied that it did not. On the basis of that assurance, the privileges were restored.

"Two catechisms in general use before 1870 verify this position. Keenan's *A Doctrinal Catechism* asks: 'Must not Catholics believe the pope in himself to be infallible?' And the answer is: 'This is a Protestant invention; it is no article of the Catholic faith; no decision of his can oblige, under pain of heresy, unless it is received and enforced by the teaching body, that is, the bishops of the Church'" (1854 ed., c. IX, p. 112). When papal infallibility was decreed by Pope Pius IX in 1870, this question and answer were quietly omitted from the catechism without note, comment or explanation. The *Catechism of the Catholic Religion* gave substantially the same reply.

"It is well known that Cardinal Newman was strongly opposed to the promulgation of the doctrine of infallibility. But having left the Church of England in order to join the Roman Church, and having given it such fulsome praise, he was powerless to prevent the change and did not have the courage to come back out of it. Shortly before the decree was issued, he wrote to a friend, comparing the impending decree with that setting forth the

Immaculate Conception, which was issued in 1854: 'As to the Immaculate Conception, by contrast there was nothing sudden, or secret, in the proposal... This has taken us all by surprise.' And on January 28, 1870, while Vatican I was in session, he wrote to Bishop Ullathorne, deploring what seemed imminent, and asked: 'What have we done to be treated as the faithful never were treated before? Why should an aggressive and insolent faction (by which he meant the Jesuits) be allowed to make the hearts of the just to mourn whom the Lord hath not made sorrowful?' It was a bitter pill for Newman to swallow, but he submitted and acknowledged papal infallibility." (L. Boettner, *Roman Catholicism,* pp. 242-243)

Having mentioned Cardinal John Henry Newman in the context of contemporary views of the events at Vatican I, it is useful to include in this study a compilation of his writings (excerpts from both official and private correspondence) to illustrate the moral quandary confronting some churchmen after the proclamation of *"Pastor Æternus"*.

Newman did not believe the definitions of Vatican I were necessary, and claimed that "hitherto, definitions *de fide* were grave assertions, not devotional outpourings." (Letter to Bishop Moriarty: 1.28.1870)

Shortly after the Council he stated: "It is a new and most serious precedent in the Church that a dogma *"de fide"* should be passed without definite and urgent cause. This to my mind is the serious part of the matter." "As far as I can see, no one is bound to believe it at the moment." (Letters 8.7.1870 and 8.8.1870)

Writing again to Bishop Moriarty he said, "The definition, if we are to suppose it legitimately passed, is producing a most untoward effect...and when people ask me categorically "Is it binding?", I don't know what to say. That *'securus iudicat orbis terrarum',* I am sure — but time has not been given to ascertain this."

At the end Newman came to the conclusion that the decrees of Vatican I had been obtained and accepted with "an imperiousness and an overbearing willfulness which has been a great scandal."

Yet Newman had hope that some day the damage would be repaired, and said with some degree of understatement: "Let us be patient, let us have faith, and a new pope and a reassembled council may trim the boat." Of course, because of the exigencies of the day the council was not reconvened, and honest men still yearn for a "trimming of the boat"!

"Till better advised nothing shall make me say that a mere majority in a council, as opposed to moral unanimity, in itself creates an obligation to receive its dogmatic decrees. This is a point of history and precedent." (7.27.1870)

Newman strongly believed that only a UNIVERSAL reception of the decrees on the part of the Church could remove the bar of lack of moral unanimity.

However, with these views clearly set in mind it is easily discerned that the seed of the contemporary doctrine of infallibility was sown somewhere in the early part of the fifteenth century, at which time three popes reigned simultaneously, each ignoring and often proclaiming "God's teaching" while contradicting the other so-called "Holy Fathers" on earth. To avoid a repetition of such a situation, some truly effective means of concentrating power in Rome was seen as both urgent and inevitable. Needless to say, Roman historians neglect to relate and are truly shamed by these historical events, which precipitated a formidable confrontation. The chronology is convoluted; however, a simple summary will register the following scenario.

For centuries before the doctrine of papal infallibility was adopted there was much difference of opinion as to where that infallibility lay. Some held that it rested in the councils speaking for the Church. Two councils, that of Constance (1415), which deposed the first pope John XXIII after he had held office for five years and had appointed several cardinals and bishops who continued to hold their offices, and that of Basle (1432), declared that "even the pope is bound to obey the councils." At another time it was held that infallibility lay in acts of the councils approved by the pope. But in 1870 it was declared to reside in the pope alone, and all good Roman Catholics now are compelled to accept that view. The Jesuits, because of their influence at the Vatican and their ability to influence the popes, also accept this. But the principal question remains: Which council pronouncement was "infallible," that of Constance and Basle? Or that of the Vatican Council? Clearly, they are contradictory and cannot both be right.

That the popes have not always been considered infallible is made clear by a review of events in the late 14th and early 15th centuries. Such a survey is given by Dr. Boettner as follows:

"In the 1300's, the popes moved to Avignon, France, and for seventy years were manifestly subservient to the French kings. This has been called the 'Babylonian Captivity' of the papacy. Following this time, Gregory XI went back to Rome. His successor, Urban VI (1378-1389) made an election promise to return to France, but election promises are not always kept, and he later refused. The French then called his election illegal and elected a new rival pope, Clement VII (1378-1394). This schism continued until a council was called at Pisa in 1409 which deposed both rival popes and elected a new one, Alexander V (1409-1410).  The rival popes refused to accept the council and so three popes were on the  scene.  After the death of Alexander V, he was succeeded by John XXIII, whom Roman Catholics do not acknowledge and whose name the present pope has taken to show the illegality of the first John XXIII.  Roman Catholics do not accept the Council of Pisa as an Ecumenical council (that is, one representative of the whole church).  But most of them accept Alexander V whom it elected! (Hefele, *History of the Church Councils,* Vol. I, p. 58).  The Council of Pisa declared that a council is superior to a pope.

"The schism continued and the Council of Constance (1414-1418) was called.  This council deposed all three popes and elected a new one, Martin V (1417-1431)… The Council of Constance also declared that a council is superior to a pope, and thus it acted to depose three popes at once.  Hefele, one of the best known Roman authorities, takes the odd position that the first forty sessions of the council were not ecumenical, but that sessions 41-45, presided over by Martin V whom they elected, were ecumenical.  Martin proceeded to confirm all the decrees of the first forty sessions except those which minimized the papacy.  Here, of course, was the pope's dilemma.  If the earlier sessions were valid, the council was supreme over the pope.  If not, the other popes were not deposed and Martin V was not rightly elected! The Vatican Council of 1870 declared: They err from the right course who assert that it is lawful to appeal from the judgement of the Roman Pontiff to an ecumenical council, as to an authority higher than that of the Roman Pontiff.' This is wonderful.  The pope is higher than a council. The Vatican Council made him so!  But a previous council, just as regular, had denied him to be so." (Article, *The Bible Presbyterian Reporter,* Dec. 195, quoted in Boettner, pp. 241-2)


It is also interesting to record that the Council of Trent, which totally defined Roman Catholic theology after the Reformation, said *not one word* about the so-called "infallibility of the popes."  This obviously proved that the theory was never accepted by the universal Church from the outset, and therefore is a strikingly novel teaching and a certain innovation in Christian thought and tradition.

As a sidelight to our study, we might recall that throughout history Church councils were convoked by emperors without the approval of, and sometimes against the wishes of the pope, and that from the year 325 (Council at Nicæa) to 580 (Council at Constantinople), among the 1,109 bishops in attendance at these Holy Synods, which defined Christian teaching for the ages, only 19 were bishops from the Western Church — and those often arrived late, unprepared, or totally ignorant of the salient issues at hand.

The Vatican Council (I) in 1870 was asked to define and vote on the "doctrine of infallibility". This raises the reasonable assumption that if a doctrine is supposed to be God-given, of sure divine mandate, how could anyone be asked to "vote" on such an issue? It is either true because God Himself has decreed it so — or it is not! Scripture is silent about infallibility; history is quiet; and the tradition of the Christian Church is also mute. A *vote* cannot decide doctrine, and certainly one may not usher in a new teaching for personal gain (or a simple craving for power) by acclamation and the manipulation of a ballot box.

If a council merely affirms the power resident in a pope, as Roman Catholic theologians are forced to teach, then a council is not really free in the sense St. Paul taught so powerfully in Galatians and First Corinthians, when he spoke of Christian truth and the supremacy of the individual conscience. To St. Paul, majority votes cannot determine right or wrong nor guarantee freedom in such a setting. Coerced councils merely become rubber stamps for a pope and his petulant curia. Nevertheless, we must raise the objection frequently posed at Vatican Council I by those who opposed a declaration of infallibility, i.e., "If the pope speaks as an oracle of the Church, with the consent of the Church, then his power is certainly not absolute." And if a council is convened to grant this "power" of infallibility, does it not reasonably follow that a council is superior to a pope by the very fact that it issues and graciously grants such authority to him?

In the same vein, we must seek why the Roman Church does not teach, nor has ever claimed, that each preceding pope has the "divine right" by virtue of his so-called role as "Vicar of Christ" to appoint a successor to himself? In effect, Christ's Vicar must hand over such authority to a council of cardinals time after time to mandate a majority vote in conclave, a consensus to the will of Almighty God.

Roman Catholic apologists make much of the fact that their Church is not a democratic institution, yet they sustain very stringent rules for a democratic vote in determining their highest elected official!

In the following rather lengthy quotation from Luis Bermejo's work on Vatican I, its obstacles and opportunities, he examines the claims of the papacy made through Vatican I, in which the Roman Church assumes divine right for her actions and the weight of history for her proclamations, neither of which even remotely support such grandiose assumptions:

"Catholic consciousness and to some extent even the present ecumenical discussion on the papacy seem to have exceedingly absolutized and, what is worse, isolated Vatican I from other councils, especially those of the first centuries. Papal claims to universal jurisdiction by divine right came up for discussion fairly early. Celestine, Leo and Vigilius tried to impose those views on the East, but Leo no more succeeded at Chalcedon than Celestine did at Ephesus and Vigilius at Constantinople II. Rome's doctrinal claims, almost fully developed by the second half of the fourth century, found no support whatever at Constantinople I, which — just as Nicæa had done earlier — acknowledged in Rome only the pre-eminence of moral, not jurisdictional authority over the universal Church; whereas the proceedings at Ephesus, Chalcedon and Constantinople II plainly show that the jurisdictional claims of Rome were unacceptable in the East, and as such, they were rejected. Vatican I absolutizes those claims and raises them to the highest level of a dogma of faith; but the contrary testimony of the first five councils cannot be bypassed. Nor can one take shelter in the fact that the dogmatization of Vatican I is the climax of a long process of dogmatic development, as if the papal views rejected by the Eastern councils were not really identical with those of Vatican I. For there is very little substantial difference between the doctrine of Celestine and particularly Leo, on the one hand, and that contained in *"Pastor æternus"* on the other. Both the popes as well as Vatican I claimed for Rome universal jurisdictional primacy by divine right, and it is this *very* contention that proved unacceptable to the Eastern councils. It may perhaps be exaggerated to say that the early councils, in a sort of pre-emptive strike, rejected in an anticipatory manner the very doctrine of Vatican I, but it cannot be denied that in their dealings with the East Celestine, Leo and Vigilius embody to a remarkable degree the *ex sese* of Vatican I, whereas the Eastern councils, particularly Ephesus, Chalcedon and Constantinople II, reflect rather the *concensus Ecclesiæ* — two clearly distinct ecclesiologies that are hard to reconcile."
(L. Bermejo, *Towards Christian Reunion,* pp. 126-127)

---

### WHAT ARE THE PROOFS? SOME RANDOM THOUGHTS

The entire weight of papal claims to divine sanction for the theory of infallibility rests, as we have seen, on the famous "Petrine passage" found in Matthew 16:18. This passage occurs only in the Gospel of St. Matthew, and its origins in history are not certain. Some scholars believe that the pericope refers to the founding of a loosely-knit, Spirit-called *ecclesia* — meaning an assembly or gathering. The word never appears in the Old

Testament and is clearly meant to denote those "called out" as believers in Christ Jesus our Lord. Those endowed with gifts of the Spirit held office, but this endowment was not confined to officials alone. All Christians are expected to be "crowned" with these gifts while using them to benefit the whole Church. In this way members participate in the "royal priesthood" and should by their lives and example declare the wonderful deeds of Almighty God to mankind. (I Peter 2:9)

What remains paramount here is that when referring to the Church, or those called out, "*Church* designates a group of people, either all the Christians in one city or those gathered for worship in one place (Acts 14:23; I Cor. 1:2; II Cor 1:1; Romans 16:5; I Cor 16:19) or all the Christians in all the Churches, the whole Church (Matt 16:18; Eph 1:22). IT NEVER SIGNIFIES A BUILDING OR DENOMINATION." (*Harper's Bible Dictionary*, p. 168)


**The Church,** as St. Paul forcefully proclaims:
**"...is one body, and one Spirit, one Lord, one Faith, one Baptism."**
(Ephesians 4:5)


Roman assertions that their Church is superior, based solely on Matthew 16:18, a passage which never occurs in the Gospel of St. Mark, is fanciful at best. For if this passage is so important and vital to the government of the Church, and the ultimate salvation of souls (as papal apologists insist), why did Peter not mention such a portentous claim in the Gospel, since St. Mark, a constant companion of Peter, wrote down everything he heard the Fisherman preach? This is all the more puzzling when we know that Papias, the great historian of the early Church, asserts:

"Mark was the interpreter of Peter and wrote carefully all that he remembered, both the words and deeds of the Lord. ...Mark had not himself heard from the Lord, but knew them from Peter's account... Mark wrote only what he remembered — taking care neither to omit or falsify." (Eusebius, *Ecclesiastical History*, III: 39, 15f.)

And John McKenzie, one of the most renowned contemporary Roman Catholic authorities on Holy Scripture, says:

"Although it is impossible to verify everything that Papias says... most modern critics find his account so much in harmony with the internal evidence of the Gospel itself that they accept the testimony... Any skepticism of early critics has now been abandoned... Peter did not know the Greek language well... therefore Mark wrote what Peter said carefully and exactly." (*Dictionary of the Bible*)

70

In the first two centuries of Christian history, we find very few traces of any use of Matthew 16:18. The meager evidence that such a use occurred is found in Justin's *Dialogue* (100.4: 106.3) and in *Pseudo-Clementina*. The latter is a forged document of historical interest, but of no lasting importance. In fact, Origen is one of the few authorities to explain the unique relationship between terms such a "Rock" and "Church" using this statement. He concludes that *"Rock means every disciple of Christ"* motivated by the Spirit who emphasizes and "confesses *that Jesus is Lord.*" (Origen, *Matthew 16:18, Discourse*)

Therefore, we are able to trace from earliest documents a rather benign interpretation of Matthew 16:18 emanating from the primitive Church — certainly nothing even approaching the later Roman exegesis. Origen knew only too well that St. Paul spoke of Christ as the "Rock of offense" (Romans 9:33), and said "for they drink of that spiritual Rock which followed them and that Rock was Christ!" (I Cor 10:4).

As for infallibility, and that it is based on Matthew 16, this doctrine was not even whispered in Church classrooms until the thirteenth century, at which time it was called the "work of Satan" by Pope John XXII and, as we have seen, was vehemently denied in Roman Catholic apologetical texts until 1870.

Perhaps it is unnecessary to return to the teachings of the Church Fathers when we have to go back so few years to see that infallibility was never affirmed in Roman Catholic catechisms; indeed, it was DENIED, barely one hundred years ago, as we witnessed in the remark of Keenan's *Catechism* and the *Catechism of Catholic Religion*.

On the question of how history was manipulated at Vatican I, L. Bermejo is candid, yet concise:

"Perhaps the main historical defect of Vatican I lies, not in the one-sided selection of testimonies in favor of papal infallibility — and this selection, as we have seen, was not particularly felicitous — but rather in the lack of a comprehensive, objective and unbiased view of papal history. This view would have called for an impartial assessment, not only of the historical instances when popes proclaimed truth as truth, but also of those when they taught error as truth. For the arbitrary selection of testimonies in favor of the magisterial office of the popes tends to distort the total picture of papal interventions in the area of truth and its proclamation. If the innumerable instances of correct papal teaching should not be minimized, neither should the cases of papal distortion of truth be passed over in silence. Maybe an excessive concentration on the case of Pope Honorius prevented the bishops of Vatican I from gaining a more comprehensive view of previous papal history, with its numerous bright spots and its sundry shadowy corners. Light and darkness are hopelessly intermingled in the popes' search for truth, and the selectivity of Vatican I, overstressing papal achievements and underplaying papal failures, is already condemned in its source. The method utilized by the council in its handling of history will hardly commend itself to the modern historian whose primary concern is not the justification of a preconceived position, but rather the objective exposition of the truth." (L. Bermejo; *Towards Christian Runion,* p. 83)

But we shall again turn to the evidence of Scripture and history (especially the absence of any proclamation by the so-called first infallible pope, Peter) in completing our study.

## TESTIMONY OF THE FATHERS

Although the incident at Cæsarea Philippi is recorded in the Gospel of St. Mark (Mk 8:27), the words to Peter appear nowhere in his account. It is an unsolved mystery why Peter, if he was the universal teacher of the entire Church in that special sense the popes describe, would not have taken care that the words so important to papal primacy appear some place in the Gospel written under his direction. Even if one was able to accept the statement of Jesus Christ to Peter at face value, it is obvious that it has nothing to do with the papacy. The testimony of the Fathers, who accurately reflected the mind of the early Church, is quite clear in this regard. Among these testimonies, we discover that:

8 held that the "Rock" was the college of apostles which Peter represented.

44 believed that the "Rock" was the faith which Peter confessed; i.e., "Thou art Christ, Son of the living God."

16 taught that the "Rock" was Jesus Christ Himself.

17 proclaimed that the "Rock" was Peter as a representative of the entire group of believers, the first Christians, or the "Church".

Origen referred to the "successors of Peter" as "the Church and the faithful." To his most authoritative commentary we must attach absolute credence as he was one of the most learned and accurate observers of that which the early Church practiced and believed. To Origen, the ROCK was not only Christ, but

"every imitator of Christ... who drank from a spiritual Rock that followed them." (Origen, *Commentary on Matthew,* XII: 10)

While Origen and others felt that the "Rock" was the Church gathered around the Lord, *not one* of the Fathers, those most perceptive and authentic translators of early thought, viewed the "Rock" as Peter, Bishop of Rome alone. It would seem that the Roman Church after 1870 stands in isolation, fighting both history and tradition, giving the pope sole authority in spiritual matters or jurisdictional rights within the religious milieu.

In fact, Cyprian, unwilling to grant even a *simple primacy* to the Bishop of Rome, considers that "the whole body of bishops is addressed in Peter." St. Cyprian rightly concludes that the "Rock is the unity of faith, not the person of Peter." (*De Catholicae Ecclesiae Unitate,* cap. 4-5)

"I believe that by the Rock you must understand the unshaken faith of the apostles." (St. Hilary, *2nd Book on the Trinity*)

St. Gregory Nazianzen, speaking of Peter, comments:
"This one (Peter) is called a rock in order that on his FAITH (Rock) he may receive the foundations of the Church." *(26th Discourse)*

St. Gregory of Nyssa in the *Panegyric of St. Stephen* asserts:
"We chiefly commemorate today those who have shone with a great and dazzling light (splendor) of piety. I mean Peter, James and John, who are the Princes of the Apostolic Order... The apostles of the Lord were stars that brightened all under heaven. Their princes and chiefs Peter, James and John whose martyrdom we celebrate, suffered in many ways... Peter received the favor of a glory suitable to his dignity... James was beheaded, aspiring to the possession of Christ, who is truly his head, for the head of man is the Christ, Who at the same time is the only Head of the Church... The apostles are the foundations of the Church, the columns and pillars of truth... from them flow abundant torrents of divine doctrine."

St. Cyril of Alexandria in *Upon St. John, Book II, Chap. xii,* says:
"The word "Rock" has only a denominative value — it signifies nothing but the steadfast and firm faith of the apostles."

In his *Letter to Nestorius,* St. Cyril says:
"Peter and John were equal in dignity and honor. Christ is the foundation of all — the unshakeable Rock upon which we are all built as a spiritual edifice."

"The disciples, disputing for primacy, were compelled by Christ's law of equality, Who said: "Ye must become as little children."

— St. Clement of Alexandria, Stromat, 5th Book, 5th section

"If you believe that God has raised the whole building of His Church on Peter alone, what will you say of John, the Son of Thunder? What will you say of each of the apostles? Will you venture to say that the gates of hell shall not prevail against Peter in particular, but shall prevail against the others... are not the words addressed to them all?"

— Origen, Commentary on Matthew

"The Church, the House of the Lord, is built upon the foundations of the faith of the apostles and prophets."

— St. Basil of Cæsarea, Second Chapter of Isaiah

It must be remembered that in all these commentaries when the writer expresses belief in the "faith of the apostles" he is saying, quite clearly, "faith in Christ." "Thou art Christ, the Son of the living God" is the *Rock* upon which the Church is founded, and that Rock reigns today when we witness to Him in our life and worship.

St. Ambrose, writing in *The Incarnation,* sums up the entire matter when he declares:

"Faith is the foundation of the Church, for it was not of the person but the faith of St. Peter of which it was said, 'the gates of hell shall not prevail'; certainly it is the confession of faith which has vanquished the powers of hell."

"Jesus Christ is the Rock. He did not deny the grace of His name... to Peter because he borrowed from the Rock the constancy and solidity of his faith — thy Rock is thy faith, and faith is the foundation of the Church. If thou art a Rock, thou shalt be in the Church, for the Church is built upon the Rock... (the profession of faith in Christ Jesus)."

**(Note:** St. Ambrose often spoke disparagingly of the Bishop of Rome as usurping the legitimate rights of other bishops in the Church. Cf. *On the Incarnation, On St. Luke,* and *On the 69th Psalm.*)

St. Augustine, one of the most renowned theologians of the Western Church, claimed by the Roman See as "Father and Doctor", says:

"In one place I said... that the Church had been built on Peter as the Rock... but in fact it was not said to Peter, "Thou art the Rock," but rather

"Thou art Peter." The Rock was Jesus Christ, Peter having confessed Him as all the Church confesses Him, He was then called Peter, "the Rock" ... (*ed.*, for his faith) ...Between these two sentiments let the reader choose the most probable." (St. Augustine, *Retractions - 13th Sermon; Contra Julianum 1:13*)

St. Augustine also adds: "Peter had not a primacy over the apostles, but AMONG the apostles, and Christ said to them "I will build upon Myself, I will not be built upon thee." *(ibid.)*

To Augustine, this made Peter somewhat less than an infallible teacher, without his fellow bishops and all the faithful by his side. It is this statement by Augustine which Pope Hadrian VI (1522-25) had in mind when he declared:

"A Pope may err alone, not only in his personal, but official capacity."

In still another letter Augustine quotes Cyprian, with whom he is in full agreement:

"For neither did Peter whom the Lord chose... when Paul afterwards disputed with him... claim or assume anything and arrogantly to himself, so as to say that he held a primacy and should rather be obeyed by newcomers..."

Finally, Augustine concludes, near the end of his earthly life, with these words on the "Rock of the Church":

"Christ said to Peter... I will build thee upon Myself, I will not be built upon thee. Those who wished to be built among men said, 'I am of Paul, I am of Apollos, I am of Cephas' — however, those who did not wish to be built upon Peter but upon the Rock say, I am of Jesus Christ." *(Retractions, 13th Sermon)*

Holy Scripture repeatedly refers to the Godhead as the "Rock" since Jesus Christ is the only foundation upon which the Church can be built. In each place of Scripture, Old and New Testaments alike, where the word "Rock" is used, we see the reference to the divinity or faith in Almighty God, certainly not Peter. *(Ex 17:6; 33:12; Deut 32:4; 32:15; 32:18; 32:31; I Sam 2:2; II Sam 22:2; 22:32; 22:47; 23:3; Ps 28:1; 31:3; 62:2; 89:26; 92:15; 95:1; Isa 17:10; I Cor 10:4)* Along with this Biblical evidence, St. Augustine says without hesitation in *Retractions:*

"The Rock is the Principal Word, that is why Peter is derived from the Rock and not the Rock from Peter."

Church historian W.H.C. Frend narrows the various interpretations with a logical and historically accurate summation:

"Petrine texts were interpreted allegorically. As we have seen, they were referred by Origen and his successors to 'the Church,' or 'the faithful,' and not to Peter himself. Commenting on Matt. 16:18, Origen stated that 'the Rock' was 'every imitator of Christ from whom they drank, who drank from the spiritual Rock that followed them.' The Church and its constitution were built on such a Rock. The passage referred to the apostles as a whole and not only to Peter. Elsewhere, Peter is seen as the pattern of all who had a right disposition for the Church to be built. The 'keys of the kingdom' were given to all who believed in the confession Peter made and repented their faults. Origen's lead was followed. In the fifth century, we find the Alexandrian Monophysite patriarch, Timothy Ælurus (454-77), writing to the Church of Constantinople and referring to Peter's Rock as 'meaning the orthodox faith,' and not Peter's successors." (W.H.C. Frend, *The Rise of Christianity,* p. 400)

Similar beliefs were held by other Church Fathers. For example, St. Hilary writes:

"The Rock *(petra)* is the blessed and only rock of the faith confessed by the mouth of Peter. It is on this Rock of the confession of faith that the Church is built." *(2nd Book on the Trinity,* St. Hilary of Poitiers, c. 315-368)

Hilary wrote the first lengthy study of the doctrine of the Church in Latin. Proclaimed a "Doctor of the Church" by the Roman See in 1851, he is called the Athanasius of the Western Church. Along with such exegesis, the Eastern Father, St. John Chrysostom, and the (Western) doctor St Jerome teach that:

"The Rock on which Christ will build His Church means the faith of confession." (St. John Chrysostom, *53rd Homily on St. Matthew)*

"Christ is the Rock Who granted to His apostles that they should be called rocks. God has founded His Church on this Rock, and it is from this Rock that Peter has been named." (St. Jerome, *6th Book on Matthew)*

In fact, so complete is the witness of the Fathers that Ignaz von Döllinger, universally acclaimed as the patron of Church history in the late nineteenth century, who left the Roman Church upon the proclamation of the doctrine of infallibility, writes with candor and certain knowledge:

"Of all the Fathers who interpret these passages in the Gospels (Matthew 16:18, et. al.) NOT A SINGLE ONE OF THEM applies these passages to the Roman bishops as Peter's successor. How many Fathers had busied themselves with these texts, yet not one of them whose commentaries we possess, Origen, Chrysostom, Hilary, Augustine, Theodoric... has dropped the faintest hint that the primacy of Peter is the consequence of the commission and promise to Peter. Not one of them has explained the Rock or foundation on which Christ will build His Church as the office given to Peter to be transmitted to his successors, but they understood by it either Christ Himself, or Peter's confession of faith in Christ, often both together. Or else they thought Peter was the foundation equally with the other apostles, the twelve being together the foundation stones of the Church." *(The Papacy and the Council,* p. 91)

So now Rome, which relies on the "witness" of history to claim jurisdiction over all believers, is shorn of any defense when she is confronted with these writings. Is it any wonder that patristics (or the study of the Fathers) is given such a minor place in Roman seminary curricula? Or can one doubt that with such massive evidence against her, the Church of Rome was forced to edit manuscripts and doctor the testimony of ancient observers in the faith?

Dr. von Döllinger claimed shortly after the First Vatican Council that Rome would forever be forced to pile one lie on top of another to support the great blasphemy of papal infallibility. How prophetic he was!

At Vatican Council I the claim was made that papal infallibility was inherent in the Church from apostolic days. This is patently untrue. There is absolutely no proof of such wild claims, and churchpersons today, Roman and non-Roman, would never make such exaggerated declarations in the company of learned men and women.

Luis Bermejo comments on the sometimes erroneous boasts of the infallibilists:

"In the light of the above it is not difficult to see that the claim of Vatican I, that in promulgating the dogma of papal infallibility the council was 'adhering to the tradition received from the beginning of the Christian faith' (DS 3073), is objectively false, for this doctrine did not exist, either explicitly or implicitly, before the end of the 13th century. Papal infallibility is not implicitly contained in the doctrine of papal primacy; in fact there is a certain tension between these two tenets of Catholic ecclesiology, for primacy of power implies certain freedom to change and innovate, whereas infallibility essentially restricts this freedom, since the Pope is bound by the infallible decisions of his predecessors. Pope John XXII perceived this tension and opted for sovereignty of power. Hence, the implied reasoning of Vatican I, that doctrinal primacy leads to or includes infallibility, remains highly questionable to say the least." *(L. Bermejo, Toward Christian Reunion)*

St. Peter, then, whom the Roman theologians would make the "apostle prince" of their Church, knew only one "supreme Shepherd," that is Jesus Christ. As for himself, Peter was the brother of the Lord with the other apostles by his very ministry. Peter never spoke of his "primacy" or "sovereignty". He never raised himself above the other pastors of the Church, whom he always addressed as equals and brothers (Acts 15:7, 3:17, 2:29, 1:16). Peter justifies any leadership as a position of love and counsel since he was an observer of the deep sufferings of Our Lord and was an eyewitness, with James and John, to the future glory of Christ (Luke 9:28-36).

There is *not one* text in Holy Scripture which denies Christ's unique role as the sole head of the Church, and there is *not one* passage where the Church is represented as anything but one body, composed of faithful as well as pastors. Therefore it is indisputable that the Power of the Keys was given to the apostles as a group. Recent Biblical research affirms more and more that any claim by one bishop in the Church to have a unique relationship with God or usurp powers which are given to other bishops is not only very bad theology, but extremely poor historical reasoning. (Cf. Matt 28:16-20; John 20:19-23)

> **"The entire world knows how profitable this fable of Christ has been to us and ours."**
> **—Pope Leo X (1513-1521)**

The official statement of belief of the Roman Church is the Creed of Pius IV. A section of that creed states:

"I also admit Holy Scripture according to that sense which Holy Mother Church has held and does hold, to whom it belongs to judge of the true sense and interpretation of the Holy Scriptures. Neither will I ever take and interpret them otherwise than according to the unanimous consent and teachings of the Fathers." *(Injunctum Nobis,* Nov. 13, 1564; modified 1887)

St. Ignatius Loyola:

*"If children make a good first communion, they will be submissive to the pope forever. Like the stick in the hands of a traveller, they shall have no personal will, no thought of their own." (Literature Depository, 1886, London)*

"If the pope errs by commanding vices or forbidding virtues, the Church *must believe* that vices are good and virtues bad, unless one wants to sin against conscience." (Robert Bellarmine, *De summo pontifice, liber IV, cap. 5, 87*) [Robert Bellarmine, a cardinal of the Roman Church, although seeming to give absolute power by such words, did not believe the pope to be *the* "leader of the Christian Church" (*ibid.*, liber V, cap. 3).

*"The pope is the meeting point between God and man...who can judge all things and be judged by no one."* —*Pope Innocent III*

Pope Clement VI (1342-52) demanded that Catholics in Armenia believe that the pope, as Vicar of Christ on earth, "possessed the same full powers which Christ had on earth."

Canon 1404 (of the Roman Catholic Church) claims that "Rome is the First See" and "judged by no one." This is a famous forgery from the time of Pope Symmachus (498-514) and omits the words "unless he is found straying from the faith," which severely limit the power of the Bishop of Rome.

---

"It should be clear that THE ONLY HEAD OF THE CHURCH, THE ONLY HEAD OF THE BODY OF CHRIST WHICH IS THE CHURCH, IS OUR SAVIOR AND HIM ALONE. It is not fitting to say of the Roman Pontiff what one says of Christ, that he (the pope) is the "head of the Church." —Maximos IV, Patriarch of the Eastern Catholic Church (under Rome)

---

# PART TWO

*Note:* The Vatican archives which were closed to scholars for centuries reopened for a brief period in the late 1960's. Access to material there was responsible for the publication of several scholarly works (published in the decade from 1965-75) which seriously damaged the theory of an infallible pope.

Claims by the Bishop of Rome that he, by his teaching authority, preserves an UNCHANGING TRADITION OF TRUTH are simply false. Any objective study of the papacy would show that through the centuries popes have decreed one thing, while their successors decreed another in contra-distinction to the original. Therefore, any study of the papacy would be incomplete without a short addendum highlighting the numerous innovations made by Roman popes in doctrine and discipline throughout the centuries, innovations which today stand discredited and empty.

By these examples we see that Roman popes *have not* handed down an unbroken chain of teaching and practice over the centuries. Dogmas have been "refined," or, as the theologians say, "developed" within the Roman fold, *new* teachings "added" (i.e., Immaculate Conception 1854, the Assumption 1950, purgatory, indulgences) for opportunistic, not theological, reasons, while pronouncements have been changed or modified on whim, not principle. A few examples follow in the Epilogue.

*"During the election of Pope Damasus I in 366 A.D., a total of 137 corpses littered the yard of the Liberian Basilica after a pitched battle between followers of Damasus, and those of his arch-rival for the papal throne, Ursinus. Other popes elected amid most violent elections were Honorius II, Celestine IV and Innocent IV... while most of the more peaceful appointments were made by the emperor, Gothic and Frankish kings, or the powerful matronae (wealthy matrons) of Rome." (Frend, History of Christianity)*

## THE EPILOGUE

In this epilogue we have included brief historical facts which show the various mutations in Roman teaching and practice, many initiated by popes themselves, over the centuries. To Rome, these changes help make up the so-called "chain of unending truth" but even the most casual observer will recognize them for what they are, definite subjective responses to the tenor of the times. After having read these brief accounts, one is able to discern that the Roman bishop often "adjusted" doctrinal teaching and disciplinary practice to suit both his own pleasure and particular situation. Although the pronouncements in each case are not necessarily "infallible" in the formal sense, since the pope was considered the "universal teacher" of the Church, the declarations take on dreaded significance when signed by his hand.

Popes see themselves as above the councils of the Church and "immune" from their decisions — unless the pope ratifies such agreements himself. At least that's what churchmen would have you think. However, in 1415 at the Council of Constance (Konstanz) in Germany, a serious, yet intriguing development arose. At this time there were three men all claiming rightful "succession" as the Bishop of Rome. This was the much discussed "Western Schism" (or Babylonian Captivity), lasting for over sixty years, the history of which has been discussed previously in this study. However, a brief glance at the schism's background would show that there were three popes reigning "gloriously" at this time, each supported by a retinue of faithful. They were "Pope John XXIII" (not to be confused with a twentieth century pope of the same name), "Pope Urban VI", and "Pope Clement VII". (The scenario becomes very complicated; other names "elected" during this time were Alexander V; Benedict XIII.) After years of in-fighting and mutual excommunications, the Council of Constance was convened to decide once and for all the serious issue of who was the rightful pope. Following months of debate, the council deposed all three of these claimants to the papal throne and elected Martin V in 1417. Without doubt, the Council of Constance by this action showed itself superior to the pope(s) who claimed total supremacy over the Church. During ensuing years, however, Roman theologians using unbelievable mental gymnastics proclaimed that "No council of the Church is superior to the dictates of the pope," clearly manipulating history for their own ends. In what could be called the ultimate act of thanklessness, Pope Martin later repudiated the very council which elected him!

In theory, at least, what the popes proclaim is "unyielding and unchangeable teaching" of the Church; in practice, it is not. Popes have often proclaimed on their own initiative a number of teachings as "illegal" or "against the will of God" which were later accepted as *de facto* Roman polity. The most glaring of these "unending teachings," "traditional" practices or disciplines which have changed or been mutated over the centuries are abstracted here.

(1) The words of the Nicene Creed were altered by Rome under pressure from Emperor Henry II. Pope Benedict VIII appended "and the Son" (the famous *filioque*) in the year 1014 in patent violation of Scripture (see John 15:26), while the manner in which it was inserted was clearly illegal.

(2) By the early twelfth century, Hugh of St. Victor, following the pattern set by St. Augustine, insisted that there were "thirty sacraments" and was allowed to remain a respectable theologian in the Occidental Church. As of this time, the Church still had not determined the number of sacred rites, and it was only with the publication of Peter Lombard's *Sentences* in the mid-twelfth century that the actual numeration of sacraments was fixed at seven.

(3) Today, Thomas Aquinas is considered the major theologian of the Roman Church. Yet his works were condemned by popes and proclaimed heretical in 1277. The Franciscans were forbidden to read his works, and it was not until years later that Thomas' teaching gained respectability. Subsequently, his works were selected by the Roman See as normative and worthy of merit.

(4) From the late fourth century, well into the eleventh, the bishops in Gaul, Spain and North Africa turned to the Bishop of Milan, an annoying rival of Rome, when they needed assistance in settling intramural disputes. At the election of St. Ambrose as Bishop of Milan, now revered in the Western and Eastern Churches, Siricius, pope at Rome, wrote: "Can no one suitable be found among the clergy? Must a layman be elected to shame the Church?" (Ambrose was not yet baptized at his *election* as bishop.)

(5) Pope John XXII (1323) proclaimed that Franciscan poverty was heretical, and those practicing it were forever excommunicated from the Roman fold. (*"Cum inter nonnullos"*) His predecessor Nicholas III had asserted that the doctrine of the poverty of Christ was the "true doctrine, the denial of which was heresy." (*"Exiit qui seminat."*)

(6) All popes from 1415 into the twentieth century declared that the reception of the Eucharist under the forms of bread and wine was clearly against the will of Almighty God. (Today this is common practice in the Roman Church.) In 1377, Pope Gregory XI excommunicated the English theologian John Wyclif for saying that the Church is the "People of God." (Note: During the conciliar years 1962-5, Vatican II in countless passages referred to the custody of the Church residing in the hands of "the People of God".)

(7) Pope Pius V (1566-1572) claimed that all "Huguenots (or **French** Protestants) should be "exterminated." This is now explained away **by** historians claiming that such was a personal "opinion" of the pope, therefore not infallible. Regardless, it remains an official utterance of the "Vicar of Christ"!

(8) In 1642, Pope Urban VIII declared that the earth was the center of the universe, and as such was the "unending teaching of the Church".

(9) John Hus (1374-1415) was condemned and burned at the stake because he taught openly that neither pope nor cardinal could establish doctrine contrary to Holy Scripture. He also was one of the first to condemn indulgences, and asked that the chalice be offered to the people at the Eucharist. (Please refer to Bishop Strossmayer's speech; cf. Appendix.)

Defenders of the papacy will say that such proclamations were not infallible, and they are right, to a point. However, one can search high and low, ask any priest or bishop in the Roman Church, check any textbook, and he will be unable to find a *list* of infallible teachings, since none exists. Some have estimated that there are anywhere from one to sixteen, but that is a presumption. We know that there is only one "official" infallible proclamation — that of the Assumption of Mary into heaven which was formally proclaimed in 1950, and possibly the very proclamation of infallibility itself. While researching this study, I approached seven different agencies of the Roman Catholic Church; *NOT ONE* WAS ABLE TO PRODUCE A LIST OF INFALLIBLE PRONOUNCEMENTS OF POPES! In fact, one priest mentioned that he had never thought of the question and, now that he did, was amazed that "it had never occurred to (him) before."

We have seen that popes taught heresy — Honorius, Liberius, Callistus, Zozimus, Vigilius; yet we have not even begun to touch on the grossly immoral lives of the popes through the ages. This alone would take a volume much larger than the one you now have in your hand. However, this legacy of popes does not directly concern us here. What does concern us is that these same men claim the place of God on earth — for what else in the view of Rome is a Vicar of Christ?

Historical support, as we have seen, is almost totally lacking in the case of *"Pastor æternus"*, the proclamation of papal infallibility by Vatican Council I. As such, the conciliar documents turn to three previous councils for definition and support. This is a most curious tactic to be sure, for there is certainly nothing in those previous assemblies to lend support for the new dogma.

Luis Bermejo relies on the testimony of Pope John VIII and the *Decretum* (IV, # 76,77) of the same pontiff.

"*Pastor æternus* finds historical support for papal infallibility in three previous ecumenical councils:  Constantinople IV (869-70), Lyons II (1274) and Florence (1439).  As regards the first, its ecumenical character is seriously challenged today on the ground of new historical evidence apparently not available in 1870.  Constantinople IV, which deposed Photius in 869, was not received by the incumbent of the Roman See, Pope Adrian, and was explicitly rejected by his successor John VIII: 'We define that...the holy council held in Constantinople...against the most holy patriarch Photius should be condemned and abolished, and should not be called council at all.'  In his letter to the papal legates at the subsequent council of 879-88 which restored Photius, Pope John repeated the condemnation: 'You will state that...we cancel from the list of holy Synods those held in Rome and Constantinople against Photius under Pope Adrian." (*Towards Christian Reunion*, p. 79)

Many times throughout history, popes have made judgements for the Roman Church which later proved to be false, deeply offensive to other faiths, or an embarrassment.  Many have been Scripturally unsound, in certain error, or both.  Among statements which are viewed as blatantly erroneous are those made by:

(1)  Pope Pius VII (1800-1823), who said in the letter *Magno et Acerbo* that he was "greeted with great and bitter sorrow" at learning that there  was a "pernicious plan, by no means the first, whereby the most sacred books of the Bible were being spread everywhere in every vernacular tongue," i.e., the language of the people.

(2) Pius cited the constitutions of previous popes who said very much the same things:  e.g., Innocent III, Pius IV, Clement VIII and Benedict XIV, on behalf of the belief that "if Scripture would be easily opened to all, it would become cheapened and exposed to contempt."  Pope Leo XIII in the encyclical *Ubi Primum* warned against the "Bible Societies which were boldly spreading through the whole world... spurning the traditions of the Holy Fathers and the Council of Trent, and aiming with all strength to translate the sacred books into the common tongue of every nation."

**In other words, these six popes, "Vicars of Jesus Christ," warned the faithful to be on guard against reading Sacred Scripture in a language they would understand.**

One of the most egregious documents of the Roman Catholic Church in recent times is the infamous *Syllabus of Errors* propagated by Pope Pius IX in 1864. Written as a series of propositions, it opposed certain novelties and modern teachings which the Church found dangerous and condemnable. It has never been retracted or disowned by Rome, although its contents are now kept closeted. The *Syllabus* boldly claimed that the Roman Church had:

"the power to employ force, or any temporal power direct or indirect," when dealing with persons dangerous to the Roman Catholic faith (#24); that it is pernicious *to deny* that the Roman Church had "immunity from civil law or its penalties," and that "the ecclesiastic court for the temporal causes of clerics must be maintained, even against the will of the state." (#31)

Furthermore, the *Syllabus* demanded that the "Roman Church be regarded as the only religion of the state, to the exclusion of all other religions" (#77) and solemnly concludes that it is "against the will of God to ask the Roman Pontiff to reconcile himself to progress, liberalism, or modern civilization." Later, the *Syllabus* reiterated the Church's stand against Bible Societies which were "placing the Bible in the hands of common people in a local language."

The *Syllabus* echoed another set of papal condemnations, issued in the Bull *Unigenitus* (1713) by Clement XI. This bull taught that

### IT IS WRONG TO SAY THAT:

**"It is necessary and useful, at every time, at every place, and for every kind of person to study and appreciate the spirit, piety and mysteries of the Holy Scriptures." (#79)**

and stated without hesitation that the "obscurity of the Word of God" is a reason to keep the "laity" from reading Holy Scripture." (#80)

Once again, Rome shows its mettle by insisting that the study of Scripture is dangerous to the "faithful." In very simple words, restrict the Bible from the hands of those who might discern the truth! For believers who find such a statement hard to believe, may we direct them to proposition #84 *(Unigenitus)* which *condemns* the "fanatics" who proclaim:

"To take away the New Testament from the hands of Christians, or to keep it closed from them… is to gag for them the mouth of Christ."

Simply put, the *Syllabus of Errors* and *Unigenitus* (never disowned by the Roman Church and listed as official teaching of the faith in the *Catholic Directory*) advocate force in dealing with "dangerous" persons who attempt putting the Bible in the hands of believers everywhere. (For verification of these documents, see *Catholic Almanac*, "Glossary", yearly editions available.) (Note: the propositions in the *Syllabus of Errors* of 1864 accompanied Pius IX's encyclical *Quanta Cura*.)

Join to these abuses other instances where the papacy supported force in dealing with anyone opposed to the Roman Church, i.e., the Crusades, Inquisition, St. Bartholomew's Day Massacre, the slaughter of Serbian Orthodox Christians in 1940-42 with over one quarter million dead, the Anabaptist murders and the wholesale execution throughout the centuries of those considered dangerous to the papacy, and it is easily seen how Rome's view of the world is grounded in its belief that "error has no rights" and is therefore subject to "control" by decree and deed.

In this short study we have seen how popes have maintained for centuries that only they have the divine right and mandate to speak for God on earth. To Rome, God converses through the mouth of one man, the pope. Current misguided ecumenism is doomed to failure since Rome will never relinquish its belief that the papacy is the "center of unity," a buzz word for total mastery. If not, then we must ask why Rome still insists that anyone leaving its fold is an "apostate" — a deviant Christian liable to everlasting punishment, since he or she rejects the pope as the arbiter of salvation.

William Herr in *This Our Church*, a study sponsored by the Thomas More Press, a Roman Catholic organization, says:
"The Council of Trent... declared in its very first doctrinal statement that the traditions which have been transmitted from generation to generation since apostolic times MUST BE ACCORDED A STATUS EQUAL TO THAT OF SCRIPTURE. This is equivalent to saying that the Church itself speaks with the same authority as the Bible does." (Wm. Herr, *This Our Church*, p. 244; 1986)
In effect, Rome has re-written and composed its own Bible by canonizing papal documents and pronouncements for all the world to hear. Those who disown the Roman Church by wit of conscience or heart are excommunicated and cast off from the "elect" because of their rejection of papal claims. Such Christians, however, simply refuse to follow dual Gospels, that of the Lord, and that of the "Holy See".
Regardless, any serious student of history will research countless examples of papal abuse and corruption through the centuries. Yet, the point of this entire essay is not whether the Bishops of Rome have been

corrupt — surely we know that for a fact; and we are also quite sure that all Churches have had more than their share of impious clerics and rogues. Yet, the corruptions of the office of the so-called "Vicar of Christ" whom the popes claim to be, the Supreme Pontiff and the teacher of the unbroken faith, are all the more glaring and unbelievable because of these exalted claims.

Brian Tierney in his outstanding study of the history of infallibility concludes: "Infallibility can be a corrosive concept in Catholic ecclesiology when all its implications are explored rigorously and audaciously." (*Origins of Papal Infallibility*, p. 209)

The words of Pope St. Gregory the Great are now vividly recalled as he castigates John of Constantinople for taking the title "Supreme Bishop" of the Church:

"I pray, I entreat you. I ask you with the greatest possible gentleness, that you my brother will resist all the flatterers who give you this erroneous title, and that you will not consent to ascribe to yourself a title as senseless as it is vainglorious." (St. Gregory, *Papal Letters*, Book 5, Letter 20.)

This same title, as we have said, condemned by the early popes as the "snare of Satan", is now the chief title of the Bishop of Rome.

---

At Vatican Council I, held in 1870, a decree proclaiming the pope "infallible" was approved by the assembled bishops of the Roman Catholic Church. Many sincere bishops opposed this doctrine for a number of reasons, but left Rome before the final vote was taken. Their opposition was never recorded, although numerous documents exist in the Vatican Archives which note their views and reasons for opposing such a proclamation.

The most moving, historically accurate, and scholastically honest speech made at that council was by Bishop Joseph George Strossmayer of Bosnia. His words were lost on dusty archive shelves for many years and are only now coming to light to haunt the Roman Catholic doctrine of infallibility. That speech, in its entirety, is reproduced below.

---

Pope Pius IX (1846-78)

On May 8, 1985, the eve of the pope's visit to the Netherlands, Fr. Edward Schillebeeckx, a Roman Catholic and one of this age's most respected theologians, not given to hysteria or wishful thinking, told a conference in Holland:

"…the hierarchical structure of the Roman Catholic Church WAS NOT WILLED BY GOD, but was the result of developments during the Medieval era;" and he added that "infallibility of the pope is a clear heresy."

Venerable Fathers and Brethren:

It is not without trembling, yet with a conscience free and tranquil before God who lives and sees me, that I open my mouth in the midst of you in this august assembly. From the time that I have been sitting here with you I have followed with attention the speeches that have been made in the hall, hoping with great desire that a ray of light descending from on high might enlighten the eyes of my understanding, and permit me to vote the canons of this Holy Œcumenical Council with perfect knowledge of the case.

Penetrated with the feelings of responsibility, of which God will demand of me an account, I have set myself to study with the most serious attention the Old and New Testaments, and I have asked these venerable monuments of truth to make known to me if the holy pontiff, who presides here, is truly the successor of St. Peter, Vicar of Jesus Christ, and the infallible doctor of the Church. To resolve this grave question I have been obliged to ignore the present state of things, and to transport myself in mind, with the evangelical torch in my hand, to the days when there was neither Ultramontanism nor Gallicanism, and in which the Church had for doctors St. Paul, St. Peter, St. James, and St. John — doctors to whom no one can deny the divine authority without putting in doubt that which the holy Bible, which is here before me, teaches us, and which the Council of Trent has proclaimed as the rule of faith and morals. I have then opened these sacred pages. Well (shall I dare to say it?), I have found nothing either near nor far which sanctions the opinions of the Ultramontanes. And still more, to my very great surprise, I find in the apostolic days no question of a pope, successor to St. Peter, and vicar of Jesus Christ, any more than of Mahomet who did not then exist. You, Monsignor Manning, will say that I blaspheme; you, Monsignor Fie, that I am mad. No, Monsignori, I do not blaspheme, and I am not mad. Now, having read the whole New Testament, I declare before God, with my hand raised to that great crucifix, that I have found no trace of the papacy as it exists at this moment. Do not refuse me your attention, my venerable brethren, and with your murmurings and interruptions do not justify those who say, like Father Hyacinthe, that this council is nothing, but that our votes have been from the beginning dictated by authority. If such were the case, this august assembly, on which the eyes of the whole world are turned, would fall into the most shameful discredit. If we wish to make it great, we must be free. I thank his Excellency,

Monsignor Dupanloup, for the sign of approbation which he makes with his head: this gives me courage, and I go on.

Reading then the sacred books with that attention with which the Lord has made me capable, I do not find one single chapter, or one little verse, in which Jesus Christ gives to St. Peter the mastery over the apostles, his fellow-workers. If Simon, son of Jonas, had been what we believe his holiness Pius IX to be today, it is wonderful that He had not said to him, "When I have ascended to my Father, you should all obey Simon Peter as you obey Me. I establish him my vicar upon earth."

Not only is Christ silent on this point, but so little does He think of giving a head to the Church, that when He promises to His apostles to judge the twelve tribes of Israel (Matt. 19:28), He promises them twelve thrones, one for each, without saying that among those thrones one shall be higher than the others — which shall belong to Peter. Certainly, if He had wished that it should be so, He would have said it. What do we conclude from this sentence? Logic tells us that Christ did not wish to make St. Peter the head of the apostolic college. When Christ sent the apostles to conquer the world, to all He gave the promise of the Holy Spirit. Permit me to repeat it: if He had wished to constitute Peter His vicar, He would have given him the chief command over His spiritual army. Christ — so says the Holy Scripture — forbade Peter and his colleagues to reign or to exercise lordship, or to have authority over the faithful like the kings of the Gentiles (St. Luke 22:25). If St. Peter had been elected pope, Jesus would not have spoken thus; but according to our tradition, the papacy holds in its hands two swords, symbols of spiritual and temporal power.

The Proclamation of the Dogma of Infallibility at First Vatican Council, July 18, 1870

90

One thing has surprised me very much.  Turning it over in my mind, I said to myself, If Peter had been elected Pope, would his colleagues have been permitted to send him with St. John to Samaria to announce the Gospel of the Son of God?  What do you think, venerable brethren, if at this moment we permitted ourselves to send his holiness Pius IX and his Excellency Mons. Plantier to go to the Patriarch of Constantinople, to pledge him to put an end to the Eastern schism?

But here is another still more important fact.  An Œcumenical Council is assembled at Jerusalem to decide on the questions which divide the faithful.  Who would have called together this council if St. Peter had been pope?  St. Peter.  Who would have presided at it?  St. Peter, or his legate.  Who would have promulgated the canons?  St. Peter.  Well, nothing of this occurred.  The apostle assisted at the council as all the others did, yet it was not he who summed up, but St. James; and when the decrees were promulgated, it was in the name of the apostles, the elders, and the brethren (Acts 15).  It it thus that we do in our Church?  The more I examine, O venerable brethren, the more I am convinced that in the Scriptures the son of Jonas does not appear to be first.

Now, while we teach that the Church is built upon St. Peter, St. Paul (whose authority cannot be doubted) says, in his epistle to the Ephesians 2:20, it is built on the foundation of the apostles and prophets, Jesus Christ Himself being the chief corner-stone.  And the same apostle believes so little in the supremacy of St. Peter, that he openly blames those who would say, We are of Paul, We are of Apollos (I Cor. 1:12), as those who say, We are of Peter.  If therefore this last apostle had been the vicar of Christ, St. Paul would have taken great care not to censure so violently those who belonged to his own colleagues.  The same apostle, counting up the offices of the Church, mentions apostles, prophets, evangelists, doctors and pastors.  Is it to be believed, my venerable brethren, that St. Paul, the great apostle of the Gentiles, would have forgotten the first of these offices, the papacy, if the papacy had been of divine institution?  The forgetfulness appeared to me to be as impossible as if an historian of this council were not to mention one word of his holiness Pius IX. *[Several voices—"Silence, heretic, silence."]* Calm yourselves, my brethren, I have not yet finished.  Forbidding me to go on, you show yourselves to the world to do wrong in shutting the mouth of the smallest member of this assembly.

I continue.  The apostle Paul makes no mention, in any of his letters directed to the various Churches, of the primacy of Peter.  If this primacy had existed, if, in one word, the Church had in its body a supreme head infallible in teaching, would the great Apostle of the Gentiles have forgotten to mention it?  What do I say?  He would have written a long letter on this all-important subject.  Then, as he has actually done, when the edifice of the Christian doctrine is erected, would the foundation, the key of the arch, be forgotten?  Now, unless you hold that the Church of the apostles was heretical (which none of us would either desire or dare to say), we are obliged to confess that the Church has never been more beautiful, more pure, or more holy, than in the days when there was no pope. *[Cries of, "It is not true; it is not true."]*  Let not Monsignor di Laval say, "No," since if any of you, my venerable brethren, should dare to think that the Church which has today a pope for its head is more in the faith, more pure in its morals than the *Apostolic Church,* let  him say it openly in the face of the universe, for this enclosure is the center from which our words fly from pole to pole.

I go on.  Neither in the writings of St. Paul, St. John, nor St. James, have I found a trace or germ of papal power.  St. Luke, the historian of the missionary labors of the apostles, is silent on this all-important point.  The silence of these holy men, whose writings make part of the canon of the divinely-inspired Scriptures, has appeared to me burdensome and impossible, if Peter had been pope, and as unjustifiable as if Thiers, writing the history of Napoleon Bonaparte, had omitted the title of emperor.

I see here before me a member of the assembly, who says, pointing at me with his finger, "There is a schismatic bishop who has got among us under false colors."  No, no, my venerable brethren, I have not entered this august assembly as a thief, by the window, but by the door like yourselves. My title of bishop gives me a right to it, as my Christian conscience forces me to speak and to say that which I believe to be true.

What has surprised me most, and what moreover is capable of demonstration, is the silence of St. Peter.  If the apostle had been what we proclaim him to be — that is, the Vicar of Jesus Christ on earth— he surely would have known it; if he had known it, how is that not once did he act as pope? He might have done it on the day of Pentecost, when he pronounced his first sermon, but did not do it; neither in the two letters directed to the Church. Can you imagine such a pope, my venerable brethren, if St. Peter had been pope?  Now, if you wish to maintain that he was the pope, the natural consequence arises that you must maintain that he was ignorant of the fact. Now I ask whoever has a head to think and a mind to reflect, are these two suppositions possible?

To return, I say, while the apostle lived, the Church never thought that there could be a pope; to maintain the contrary, all the sacred writings must be entirely ignored.

But it is said on all sides, Was not St. Peter at Rome? Was he not crucified with his head down? Are not the pulpits in which he taught, the altars at which he said mass, in the Eternal City? St. Peter having been at Rome, my venerable brethren, rests only on tradition; but, if he had been Bishop of Rome, how can you from that episcopate prove his supremacy? Scaliger, one of the most learned of men, has not hesitated to say that St. Peter's episcopate and residence at Rome ought to be classed with ridiculous legends. *[Repeated cries, "Shut his mouth, shut his mouth; make him come down from the pulpit."]*

Venerable brethren, I am ready to be silent; but is it not better, in an assembly like ours, to prove all things, as the apostle commands, and to hold fast what is good? We have a dictator, before whom we — even his holiness Pius IX himself — must prostrate ourselves, and be silent and bow our heads. That dictator is history. This is not like a legend, which can be made as the potter makes his clay, but is like a diamond which cuts on the glass what cannot be cancelled. Till now I have only leant on her; and if I have found no trace of the papacy in the apostolic days, the fault is hers, not mine. Do you wish to put me into the position of one accused of falsehood? You may do it, if you can.

I hear from the right someone expressing the words — "Thou art Peter, and on this rock I will build my Church." I will answer this objection presently, my venerable brethren; but, before doing so, I wish to present you with the result of my historical researches.

Finding no trace of the papacy in the days of the apostles, I said to myself, I shall find what I am in search of in the annals of the Church. Well, I say it frankly — I have sought for a pope in the first four centuries, and I have not found him. None of you, I hope, will doubt the great authority of the holy Bishop of Hippo, the great and blessed St. Augustine. This pious doctor — the honor and glory of the Catholic Church, was secretary in the Council of Melvie. In the decrees of this venerable assembly are to be found these significant words — "Whosoever wills to appeal to those beyond the sea shall not be received by any one in Africa to the communion." The bishops of Africa acknowledge the bishop of Rome so little that they smote with excommunication those who would have recourse to an appeal. These same bishops, in the Sixth Council of Carthage, held under Aurelius, Bishop of that city, wrote to Celestinus, Bishop of Rome, to warn him not to receive appeals from the bishops, priests, or clerics of Africa; and that he should send no more legates or commissaries; and that he should not introduce human pride into the Church.

That the Patriarch of Rome had from the earliest times tried to draw to himself all the authority is an evident fact; but it is an equally evident fact that he had not the supremacy which the Ultramontanes attribute to him. Had he possessed it, would the bishops of Africa — St. Augustine first among them — have dared to prohibit the appeals of their decrees to his supreme tribunal? I confess without difficulty that the Patriarch of Rome held the first place. One of Justinian's laws says, "Let us order, after the definition of the four councils, that the holy pope of ancient Rome shall be the first of the bishops, and that the most high Archbishop of Constantinople, which is the New Rome, shall be the second." "Bow down to the supremacy of the pope," you will say to me. Do not run so fast to this conclusion, my venerable brethren, inasmuch as the law of Justinian has written on the face of it, "Of the order of the patriarchal sees." Precedence is one thing, the power of jurisdiction is another. For example, supposing that in Florence there was an assembly of all the bishops of the kingdom, the precedence would be given to the Primate of Florence, as among the Easterns it would be accorded the Patriarch of Constantinople, as in England to the Archbishop of Canterbury. But neither the first, nor the second, nor the third, could deduce from the position assigned to him a jurisdiction over his colleagues.

The importance of the bishops of Rome proceeded not from a divine power, but from the importance of the city in which they had their seat. Monsignor Darboy (in Paris) is not superior in dignity to the Archbishop of Avignon; but, in spite of that, Paris gives him a consideration which he would not have, if, instead of having his palace on the bank of the Seine, he had it on that of the Rhone. That which is true in the religious order is the same in civil and political matters: the Prefect of Rome is not more a prefect than one at Pisa; but civilly and politically he has a greater importance.

I have said that from the very first centuries the Patriarch of Rome aspired to the universal government of the Church. Unfortunately, he very nearly reached it; but he had not succeeded assuredly in his pretensions, for the Emperor Theodosius II made a law by which he established that the Patriarch of Constantinople should have the same authority as he of Rome (*Leg. cod. de sacr., etc.*). The fathers of the Council of Chalcedon put the bishops of the New and the Old Rome in the same order on all things, even ecclesiastical (*Can. 28*). The Sixth Council of Carthage forbade all the bishops to take the title of prince of the bishops, or sovereign bishop. As for this title of Universal Bishop, which the popes took later, St. Gregory I, believing that his successors would never think of adorning themselves with it, wrote these remarkable words: "None of my predecessors has consented to take this profane name; for when a patriarch gives himself the name **of** *Universal,* the title of patriarch suffers discredit. Far be it then from Christians to desire to give themselves a title which brings discredit upon their brethren!"

The words of St. Gregory are directed to his colleague of Constantinople, who pretended to the primacy of the Church. Pope Pelagius II calls John, Bishop of Constantinople, who aspired to the high priesthood, "impious and profane." "Do not care," he said, "for the title of Universal, which John has usurped illegally. Let none of the patriarchs take this profane name; for what misfortunes may we not expect, if among the priests such elements arise? They would get what has been foretold of them — He is the king of the sons of pride" (*Pelagius II, Lett. 13*). Do not these authorities prove (and I might add a hundred more of equal value), with a clearness as the sun at mid-day, that the first bishops of Rome were not till much later recognized as universal bishops and heads of the Church? And on the other hand, who does not know that from the year 325, in which the First Council of Nicæa was held, down to 580, the year of the Second Œcumenical Council of Constantinople, among more than 1,109 bishops who assisted at the first six general councils, there were not more than nineteen Western bishops? Who does not know that the councils were convoked by the emperors without informing, and sometimes against the wish of, the Bishop of Rome? — that Hosius, Bishop of Cordova, presided at the First Council of Nicæa, and edited the canons of it? The same Hosius presided afterwards at the Council of Sardica, excluding the legates of Julius, Bishop of Rome.

I say no more, my venerable brethren; and I come now to speak of the great argument — which you mentioned before — to establish the primacy of the Bishop of Rome by the Rock (*petra*). If this were true, the dispute would be at an end; but our forefathers — and they certainly knew something — did not think of it as we do. St. Cyril in his fourth book on the Trinity says, "I believe that by the Rock you must understand the unshaken faith of the apostles." St. Hilary, Bishop of Poitiers, in his second work on the Trinity, says, "The Rock (*petra*) is the blessed and only Rock of the faith confessed by the mouth of St. Peter;" and in his Sixth book of the Trinity, he says, "It is on this Rock of the confession of faith that the Church is built." "God," says St. Jerome in his Sixth book on St. Matthew, "has founded His Church on this Rock, and it is from this Rock that the apostle Peter has been named." After him, St. Chrysostom says in his Fifty-third Homily on St. Matthew, "On this Rock I will build My Church — that is, on the faith of the confession." Now, what was the confession of the apostle? Here it is — "Thou art the Christ, the Son of the living God." Ambrose, the holy Archbishop of Milan (On the Second Chapter of the Ephesians), St. Basil of Seleucia, and the fathers of the Council of Chalcedon, teach exactly the same thing. Of all the doctors of Christian antiquity St. Augustine occupies one of the first places for knowledge and holiness. Listen then to what he writes in his Second Treatise on the First Epistle of St. John: "What do the words mean, I will build my Church on this Rock? *On this faith,* on that which said, Thou art the Christ, the Son of the living God." In his treatise on St. John we find this most significant phrase — "On this Rock which thou hast confessed I will build my Church, since Christ was the Rock." The great bishop believed so little that the Church was built on St. Peter that he said to the people in his Thirteenth Sermon, "Thou art Peter, and on this Rock (*petra*) which thou hast confessed, on this Rock which thou hast known, saying, 'Thou art Christ, the Son of the living God,' I will build my Church — upon Myself, Who am the Son of the living God: I will build it on Me, and not Me on thee." That which St. Augustine thought upon this celebrated passage was the opinion of all Christendom in his time.

Therefore, to resume, I establish: (1) that Jesus has given to His apostles the same power that He gave to St. Peter; (2) that the apostles never recognized in St. Peter the Vicar of Jesus Christ and the infallible doctor of the Church; (3) that St. Peter never thought of being pope, and never acted as if he were pope; (4) that the councils of the first four centuries, while they recognized the high position which the Bishop of Rome occupied in the Church on account of Rome, only accorded to him a pre-eminence of honor, never of power or jurisdiction; (5) that the Holy Fathers in the famous passage, "Thou art Peter, and on this Rock I will build my Church," never understood that the Church was built on Peter (*super Petrum*), but on the Rock (*super petram*), that is, on the confession of the faith of the apostle. I conclude victoriously, with history, with reason, with logic, with good sense, and with a Christian conscience, that Jesus Christ did not confer any supremacy on St. Peter and that the Bishops of Rome did not become sovereigns of the Church, but only by confiscating one by one all the rights of the episcopate. *[Voices — "Silence, impudent Protestant! Silence!]*

No, I am not an impudent Protestant. History is neither Catholic, nor Anglican, nor Calvinistic, nor Lutheran, nor Arminian, nor schismatic Greek nor Ultramontane. She is what she is — that is, something stronger than all confessions of faith of the Canons of the Œcumenical Councils. Write against it, if you dare! but you cannot destroy it, any more than taking a brick out of the Coliseum would make it fall. If I have said anything which history proves to be false, show it to me by history, and without a moment's hesitation I will make an honorable apology; but be patient, and you will see that I have not said all that I would or could; and even were a funeral pile waiting for me in the place of St. Peter's, I should not be silent, and I am obliged to go on. Monsignor Dupanloup, in his celebrated *Observations* on this Council of the Vatican, has said, and with reason, that if we declared Pius IX infallible, we must necessarily, and from natural logic, be obliged to hold that his predecessors were also infallible.

Well, venerable brethren, here history raises its voice to assure us that some popes have erred. You may protest against it or deny it, as you please, but I will prove it. Pope Victor (192) first approved of Montanism, and then condemned it. Marcellinus (296-303) was an idolator. He entered into the temple of Vesta, and offered incense to the goddess. You will say that it was an act of weakness; but I answer, a vicar of Jesus Christ *dies* rather than become an apostate. Liberius (358) consented to the condemnation of Athanasius, made a profession of Arianism, that he might be recalled from his exile and reinstated in his see. Honorius (625) adhered to Monothelitism: Father Gratry has proved it to demonstration. Gregory I (785-90) calls anyone Antichrist who takes the name of Universal Bishop, and contrariwise Boniface III (607, 8) made the parricide Emperor Phocas confer that title upon him. Paschal II (1088-99 and Eugenius III (1145-53) authorized duelling; Julius II (1509) and Pius IV (1560) forbade it. Eugenius IV (1431-39) approved of the Council of Basle and the restitution of the chalice to the church of Bohemia; Pius II (1458) revoked the concession. Hadrian II (867-872) declared civil marriages to be valid; Pius VII (1800-23) condemned them. Sixtus V (1585-90) published an edition of the Bible, and by a bull recommended it to be read; Pius VII condemned the reading of it. Clement XIV (1700-21) abolished the order of the Jesuits, permitted by Paul III, and Pius VII re-established it.

But why look for such remote proofs? Has not our holy Father here present, in his bull which gave the rules for this Council, in the event of his dying while it was sitting, revoked all that in past times may be contrary to it, even when that proceeds from the decisions of his predecessors? And certainly, if Pius IX has spoken *ex cathedra,* it is not when, from the depths of his sepulchre, he imposes his will on the sovereigns of the Church. I should never finish, my venerable brethren, if I were to put before your eyes the contradictions of the popes in their teaching. If then you proclaim the infallibility of the actual pope, you must either prove, that which is impossible — that the popes never contradicted each other — or else you must declare that the Holy Spirit has revealed to you that the infallibility of the papacy dates only from 1870. Are you bold enough to do this?

Perhaps the people may be indifferent, and pass by theological questions which they do not understand, and of which they do not see the importance; but though they are indifferent to principles, they are not so to facts. Do not then deceive yourselves. If you decree the dogma of papal infallibility, the Protestants, our adversaries, will mount in the breach, the more bold that they have history on their side, whilst we have only our own denial against them. What can we say to them when they show up all the Bishops of Rome from the days of Luke to his holiness Pius IX? Ah! if they had all been like Pius IX, we should triumph on the whole line; but alas! it is not so. *[Cries of "Silence, silence; enough, enough!"]*

Do not cry out, Monsignori! To fear history is to own yourselves conquered; and, moreover, if you made the whole waters of the Tiber pass over it, you would not cancel a single page. Let me speak, and I will be as short as it is possible on this most important subject — Pope Vigilius (538) purchased the papacy from Belisarius, lieutenant of the Emperor Justinian. It is true that he broke his promise and never paid for it. Is this a canonical mode of binding on the tiara? The Second Council of Chalcedon had formally condemned it. In one of its canons you read that "the bishop who obtains his episcopate by money shall lose it and be degraded." Pope Eugenius III (IV. in original) (1145) imitated Vigilius. St. Bernard, the bright star of his age, reproves the pope, saying to him, "Can you show me in this great city of Rome any one one would receive you as pope if they had not received gold or silver for it?"

My venerable brethren, will a pope who establishes a bank at the gates of the temple be inspired by the Holy Spirit? Will he have any right to teach the Church infallibly? You know the history of Formosus too well for me to add to it. Stephen XI caused his body to be exhumed, dressed in his pontifical robes; he made the fingers which he used for giving the benediction to be cut off, and then had him thrown into the Tiber, declaring him to be a perjurer and illegitimate. He was then imprisoned by the people, poisoned, and strangled. Look how matters were re-adjusted; Romanus, successor of Stephen, and after him, John X, rehabilitated the memory of Formosus.

But you will tell me these are fables, not history. Fables! Go, Monsignori, to the Vatican library and read Platina, the historian of the papacy, and the annals of Baronius (A.D. 897). These are facts which, for the honor of the Holy See, we should wish to ignore; but when it is to define a dogma which may provoke a great schism in our midst, the love which we bear to our venerable mother Church, Catholic, Apostolic and Roman, ought it to impose silence on us?

I go on. The learned Cardinal Baronius, speaking of the papal court, says (give attention, my venerable brethren, to these words), "What did the Roman Church appear in those days? How infamous! Only all-powerful courtesans governing in Rome! It was they who gave, exchanged, and took bishoprics; and horrible to relate, they got their lovers, the false popes, put on the throne of St Peter" (Baronius, A.D. 912). *You* will answer, These were false popes, not true ones: let it be so; but in that case, if for fifty years the see of Rome was occupied by anti-popes, how will you pick up again the thread of pontifical succession? Has the Church been able, at least for a century and a half, to go on without a head, and find itself acephalous?

Look now: The greatest number of these anti-popes appear in a genealogical tree of the papacy; and it must have been this absurdity that Baronius described; because Genebrardo, the great flatterer of the popes, had dared to say in his Chronicles (A.D. 901), "This century is unfortunate, as for nearly 150 years the popes have fallen from all the virtues of the predecessors, and have become *apostates* rather than *apostles*." I can understand how the illustrious Baronius must have blushed when he narrated the acts of these Roman bishops. Speaking of John XI (931), natural son of Pope Sergius and of Marozia, he wrote these words in his annals — "The holy Church, that is, the Roman, has been vilely trampled on by such a monster." John XII (956), elected pope at the age of eighteen, through the influence of courtesans, was not one whit better than his predecessor. I grieve, my venerable brethren, to stir up so much filth. I am silent on Alexander VI, father and lover of Lucretia; I turn away from John XXII (1319), who denied the immortality of the soul, and was deposed by the holy Œcumenical Council of Constance. Some will maintain that this council was only a private one; let it be so; but if you refuse any authority to it, as a logical sequence you must hold the nomination of Martin V (1417) to be illegal. What, then, will become of papal succession? Can you find the thread of it?

I do not speak of the schisms which have dishonored the Church. In those unfortunate days the See of Rome was occupied by two competitors, and sometimes even by three. Which of these was the true pope? Resuming once more, again I say, if you decree the infallibility of the present bishop of Rome, you must establish the infallibility of all the preceding ones, without excluding any.  But can you do that, when history is there establishing with a clearness equal to that of the sun, that the popes have erred in their teaching?  Could you do it and maintain that avaricious, incestuous, murdering, simoniacal popes have been Vicars of Jesus Christ?  Oh, venerable brethren! to maintain such an enormity would be to betray Christ worse than Judas.  It would be to throw dirt in His face.  *[Cries, "Down from the pulpit, quick; shut the mouth of the heretic!"]*

My venerable brethren, you cry out; but would it not be more dignified to weigh my reasons and my proofs in the balance of the sanctuary?  Believe me, history cannot be made over again; it is there, and will remain to all eternity, to protest energetically against the dogma of papal infallibility.  You may proclaim it unanimously; but one vote will be wanting, and that is mine!  Monsignori, the true and faithful have their eyes on us, expecting from us a remedy for the innumerable evils which dishonor the Church: will you deceive them in their hopes?  What will not our responsibility before God be, if we let this solemn occasion pass which God has given us to heal the true faith?  Let us seize it, my brethren; let us arm ourselves with a holy courage; let us make a violent and generous effort; let us turn to the teaching of the apostles, since without that we have only errors, darkness, and false traditions.  Let us avail ourselves of our reason and of our intelligence to take the apostles and prophets as our only infallible masters with reference to the question of questions, "What must I do to be saved?"  When we have decided that, we shall have laid the foundation of our dogmatic system firm and immovable on the Rock, lasting and incorruptible, of the divinely in-spired Holy Scriptures.  Full of confidence, we will go before the world, and, like the apostle Paul, in the presence of the free-thinkers, we will "know none other than Jesus Christ, and Him crucified."  We will conquer through the preaching of "the folly of the Cross," as Paul conquered the learned men of Greece and Rome; and the Roman Church will  have its glorious '89.  *[Clamorous cries, "Get down!  Out with the Protestant, the Calvinist, the traitor of the Church."]*  Your cries, Monsignori, do not frighten me.  If my words are hot, my head is cool.  I am neither of Luther, nor of Calvin, nor of Paul, nor of Apollos, but of Christ.  *[Renewed cries, "Anathema, anathema to the apostate."]*

Anathema?  Monsignori, anathema?  You know well that you are not protesting against me, but against the holy apostles under whose protection I should wish this council to place the Church.  Ah! if wrapped in their winding-sheets they came out of their tombs, would they speak a language different from mine?  What would you say to them when by their writings they tell you that the papacy had deviated from the Gospel of the Son of God, which they have preached and confirmed in so generous a manner by their blood?  Would you dare say to them, We prefer the teaching of our own popes, our Bellarmine, our Ignatius Loyola, to yours?  No, no! a thousand times, no! unless you have shut your ears that you may not hear, closed your eyes that you may not see, blunted your mind that you may not understand. Ah! if He Who reigns above wishes to punish us, making His hand fall heavy on us, as He did on Pharaoh, He has no need to permit Garibaldi's soldiers to drive us away from the eternal city.  He has only to let them make Pius IX a god, as we have made a goddess of the Blessed Virgin.  Stop, stop, venerable brethren, on the odious and ridiculous incline on which you have placed yourselves.  Save the Church from the shipwreck which threatens her, asking from the Holy Scriptures alone for the rule of faith which we ought to believe and to profess.  I have spoken:  may God help me!

Joseph Georg Strossmayer,
bishop of Diakovar (Croatia)

**Note:** Bishop Strossmayer returned to his diocese under much pressure to recant and declare submission to the pronouncements of Vatican I. "I'd rather die," he protested in a letter of 1871, "than go against my conscience and convictions." However, with intolerable pressure from Rome, and the denial of the most basic spiritual rights to his people, he made peace with Pope Pius IX in 1875. "I am doing so out of love for my people," he said. Strossmayer did not formally succumb until the end of his life, when he made a "declaration of sorts" to be obedient to the Church. He never assented to the dogma of infallibility, but simply published the required decree throughout his diocese, omitting certain passages which he knew to be untrue.

Much has been made by the infallibilists of the fact that bishops who were once opposed to the decree *"Pastor æternus"* were easily persuaded to accept the dogma once the council ended. Many bishops, it is true, did publish the decree in their respective dioceses; however, the reasons for their ultimate "acceptance" are both varied and convoluted. Much of what appeared to be simple assent belied an almost inhuman pressure to conform forced upon the bishops by Rome herself. Externally they acquiesced; however, internally, they did not believe in the new dogma.

A few examples would most certainly include Archbishop Kenrick of St. Louis, "the stiffest opponent of the definition." On January 2, 1871, he stated publicly: "The motive of my submission is simply and singly the authority of the Roman Catholic Church… (my submission) is reasonable obedience." But even then he would not teach the new dogma and "would not believe in it." (Lord Acton's letter to Dollinger, 12.23.1870)

English Bishops Clifford and Brown justified their "submissions" in much the same way as did many of the French minority bishops. For French Bishop Ramadie, and others, felt they wanted to make a simple act of obedience to the pope without expressing an opinion on the dogma. Archbishop Darboy of Paris insisted that the new dogma was false, his submission merely external, not implying an acceptance in faith. (Hasler, *"Unfehlbarkeit"*, p. 492, n. 4) Bishops David and Colet followed the same *"restricto mentalis"*.

Bishop Hefele thought that the possibility of schism in the Roman Church was a greater evil than merely publishing the decrees. To him the negative votes and the abstentions were more than enough proof to any thinking person that the council was invalid. His eventual "submission" therefore was based on a traditional principle of accepting the definition, not the arguments used to support it. Archbishop Connolly of Halifax and Bishop Place of Marseille considered the stability of the Church and the prevention of a formal schism more important than the dogma itself. (Place's letter to his clergy 8.4.1870, and Connolly's letter to Lord Acton, 6.30.1870)

Cardinal Schwarzenberg of Prague "did not believe in the new dogma and has never demanded it from anyone." (Hasler, *Unfehlbarkeit"*, p. 501) Those who could not in conscience accept the decrees, or teach them, suffered excommunication, including twenty theologians in Germany, two thirds of all Catholic historians in German universities, three French theologians, and thousands of laypersons throughout the Catholic world.

# ADDENDUM

Printing a work such as this is an on-going process.  Hopefully, after a time, we will be able to publish an appended edition containing new material gleaned over the ensuing months.

Both space and economics mandate that much material would have to remain unpublished for the time being.  However, it will eventually be brought to light.  Yet even now, from our ever-expanding library of primary sources, we are adding several bits of information which are relevant to the case in point, the case of papal infallibility, and its very belated arrival on the Roman Catholic scene.

Recently, the Rev. John Neuhaus, Director of the Center on Religion and Society headquartered in New York City, appeared on "Firing Line", a production of Wm. F. Buckley, conservative publisher, writer and lecturer.  The questioning came around to papal infallibility and the position of Joseph Cardinal Ratzinger, Prefect of the Sacred Congregation for the Doctrine of the Faith, the all-powerful curial department which "safeguards the doctrine of faith and morals" in the Roman Catholic Church.

Neuhaus commented:

"Well, one thing that was wrong with raising the question of infallibility and which doctrines are infallible, and which aren't, is that as Ratzinger himself made very clear, he said, 'Infallibility is a very late concept in Roman Catholic teaching.' It was only Vatican Council I in 1870—right?—that defined infallibility.  Thankfully it has not been put to the test very much as to exactly what it means.  Because theologically it's very embarrassing also to Roman Catholics and also to — again in the hope of not offending him — I think Cardinal Ratzinger has indicated some uneasiness about it.  To lift that up, as Fr. Curran did, as 'the' text now of how we are going to organize our theological discourse is to put front center stage a highly doubtful, certainly controverted concept called infallibility instead of keeping front center stage Jesus Christ...' *(page 19, transcript of the Dec. 10th, 1987 "Firing Line" program)*

Obviously, Cardinal Ratzinger understands the very tenuous foundations of the doctrine of papal infallibility as defined by the Roman Catholic Church.  As the present prefect of what was once called the "Holy Office" the cardinal's words strike deep and hard.

However, all relevant material on this subject is not as recent.  The following thoughts from Nilus Cabasilas, Archbishop of Thessalonica, ring out from centuries past, as interpreted by John Meyendorff, Orthodox theologian:

"The works of Nilus Cabasilas, an uncle of the famous Nicholas Cabasilas, who became Archbishop of Thessalonica a few months before his death, are directly dependent on the writings of Barlaam.  Usually he simply repeats the expressions of the Calabrian 'philosopher' with some additional developments.  Thus, he also mentions the two distinct privileges of the pope:  the Roman episcopacy and universal primacy.  Like Barlaam he sees the origin of the primacy in the *Donatio*

*Constantini*, the 28th Canon of Chalcedon and the legislation of Justinian. But he insists, using some new terms, on the more general problem of Peter's primacy. 'Peter,' he writes, 'is at the same time apostle and chief ($\H{\epsilon}\xi\alpha\rho\chi o\varsigma$) of the apostles, while the pope is neither an apostle (the apostles having ordained pastors and teachers, but not apostles) nor the Coryphæus of the apostles. Peter is a teacher of the whole world...while the pope is but the Bishop of Rome... Peter ordains the Bishop of Rome, but the pope does not nominate his successor.' To some Latins who say that 'the pope is not the bishop of a city...but simply bishop, being different in this from the others,' Nilus answers that Orthodoxy does not know bishops that would be 'simply bishops', the episcopal dignity being directly connected with concrete functions in a local Church.

"In the light of such a doctrine of the Church, Nilus interprets the words of Christ to Peter. If the pope is the successor of Peter, inasmuch as he keeps the true faith, it is clear that the words of Christ concerning Peter no longer apply to him when he loses this faith. The true faith, however, can be preserved by other bishops; it is therefore obvious that the Church of Rome is not the only one built on the Rock... The Church of Christ is established on the 'theology' of Peter, i.e., on his confession of Christ as God", but all those who have the true faith profess this very theology. Nilus understands Matt. 16:18 in the manner of Origen: every true believer is a successor of Peter, but, distinct in this from the Alexandrian theologian, he accepts the full significance of the visible structures of the Church. Origenist exegesis is thus integrated into an organic and sacramental ecclesiology. The guardians of truth and the successors of Peter are for him, as for Barlaam, the heads of the Churches, i.e., the bishops. Each member of the Church is, to be sure, firmly rooted on the Rock, but precisely to the extent that he belongs to the ecclesiastic organism, of which the bishop is head. 'There is nothing great in the see of Rome being called the apostolic throne, for each bishop is seated on the throne of Christ and is vested with a dignity higher than that of the angels.'" (*The Primacy of Peter in the Orthodox Church*, pp. 24-25)

In the text of this work, Hans von Campenhausen, the historian par-excellence of the Church's earliest history, is mentioned many times. This is due solely to the indisputable fact that he, after spending most of his life in research and study, is considered THE authoritative voice on the history of the primitive Church, the Church of the apostolic era. In his outstanding work, *Ecclesiastical Authority and Spiritual Power in the Church of the First Three Centuries*, von Campenhausen investigates the structure and theology of the earliest hierarchical milieu. Several of his more cogent observations are reprinted here.

In discussing the role of clergy and hierarchy, which should first be one of service, prayer and study of God's Holy Word, Origen, that early observer of the primitive Church, feels the hierarchy is much to bent on self-serving concerns rather than spiritual ideals.

Von Campenhausen discusses the dichotomy regarding the priestly ideal vs. actual practice in reference to Origen's observations:

"This should be the real task of Christians in authority. But how do the Church's clergy appear in reality when measured against such an ideal? Most of the bishops, says Origen, are completely lacking in understanding of their proper vocation. Instead of acting as religious examples and sympathetic physicians of the soul to their congregations, they are worldly minded, pursue earthly occupations and affairs, long for wealth and land, are haughty, quarrelsome and self-assertive, allow themselves to be flattered and corrupted, and are often less particular in the conduct of their business than secular officials. As the men in charge of penance they are alternately harsh and impermissibly complaisant, and if anyone tries to bring them to book for their sins, they form cliques, and if need be anti-churches, which keep them in office. None asks what is his true spiritual calling. A real cleric would refuse ecclesiastical honors, or accept them only when, after prayer and supplication, God had made it unmistakably clear to him that this was His will. But as things are, the most sordid methods of intrigue and demagogy are brought into play as soon as there is a chance of snatching an office, especially the highest and most lucrative office, that of bishop. Clergy brag about their seniority, and try to ensure that their children or relatives will succeed them. Such clergy are in fact serving Pharaoh rather than God. These 'tyrants' will not take advice even from their equals, much less from a layman or a pagan. The only things they take seriously are their advantages and privileges, just like the Pharisees of old — it is in Origen's writings that this comparison appears for the first time in Church history.

"The picture thus unrolled of the moral conditions of the clergy is a gloomy one. Origen knows that he may give offence with his accusations; but he takes nothing back, he waters nothing down. It is the sacred duty of the Church's teachers to secure a hearing for God's word in all the fierceness of its condemnation, and not to shrink from the trials and sufferings which may result from so doing. In evaluating his charges, of course, it is important not to lose sight of the hortatory nature of a penitential sermon, and generalize too hastily. Origen is not writing a Church Order, but giving a practical exegesis of the Scriptures, intended to improve and instruct. Not at bottom does he himself regard the mournful examples which he censures as the rule but as the exception, even if a very frequent one. If we compare his concrete details with the more cautious and reticent warnings of the Didascalia, then here and there we see the same fundamental dangers and temptations. The decisive factor which makes Origen's overall assessment markedly the more pessimistic is not so much his own external circumstances or the differences in temperament between the two writers, but the basically different standard by which Origen measures his churchmen." *[(Homilies: Genesis; Numbers; Exodus; Origen); Commentaries: Origen)]*


Cyprian, another early and reliable reporter of the primitive Church, is also discussed, and von Campenhausen sees him as a man possessed of great respect for, and confidence in, the episcopal office.                                                    .

"Cyprian *believes* in the episcopate, just as he believes in the Catholic Church. However much he may be conditioned by organizational and political considerations, and however important it may be to him to establish a clear juristic confirmation of his position, the Church itself, which he serves, and the office which supports and empowers him in this service, are for Cyprian no merely juristic entities. They are divine, sacred realities given to men, and in their vital power one not only must but ought to have complete confidence.

"That Cyprian was no 'Papalist' is well known; the Roman claims with which he had to contend, but which unfortunately cannot be very precisely determined, remain for this century anyhow completely isolated and without discernible effects. But Cyprian was also no 'conciliarist', in the constitutional sense of the word familiar in the later Middle Ages.

"We may say that in the Cyprianic conception of the relationship of mutual love between the bishops a definite element from the primitive Christian concept of the Church lives on. The belief in freedom, a belief based on faith in the power of that Christian truth in which Christians as members of Christ at all times have their being, and which yet has constantly to be triumphantly demonstrated afresh to be the truth, is no longer a real option for the mass of Christians; but it is still valid for the leaders of the Church, the group of bishops through whom the Holy Spirit works, and who in their proceedings continue to represent the totality of Church members.

"Each individual bishop exercises the full episcopate; nevertheless, it does not belong to him alone, but he possesses it only in solidarity with all the other holders of the office, with whom he is on an equality in 'honor and power'. This is particularly emphasized in the controversy over heretic baptism with the Bishop of Rome, who had boasted of his special succession from Peter, and on the grounds that he possessed a higher status than that of his episcopal colleagues had wished to dictate a decision on the question. This, however, is nothing more than insolent presumption, and a folly against which Cyprian makes a solemn protest in a great council of the African Church. In fact, at this council Cyprian, as Bishop of Carthage, and by virtue of his intellectual superiority, played a commanding role throughout, and to this extent operated himself as an African 'Pope'. Cyprian nevertheless attaches the greatest importance to the fact that the following which he acquired there was at all times entirely voluntary; it came about simply through unanimity on the question at issue, not as a result of pressure or demands from his side. As president of the council he underlines the fact that in the true Catholic Church there is no tyrannical 'compulsion', no regulations laid down by an individual to which others must conform, and also no arriving at conciliar decisions by majority votes. Each bishop has equal rights and is free without hindrance to express his opinion and, so far as he individually is concerned, to act accordingly. Christ alone will be his judge. The Church does not collapse just because here and there alternative practices are in use; but she would disintegrate if the peace and cohesion of the episcopate were to be destroyed by this—or, to be more precise, the man who sought to do this would thereby place himself outside their holy covenant of love, and thus outside the one, indivisible Church." (*ibid., von Campenhausen*, chap. xi)

Recently, in his newly published work, *The Vicars of Christ: The Dark Side of the Papacy"* [Bantam Press, 1988], Peter De Rosa, graduate of the world-renowned "Gregorianum" in Rome, professor of ethics at Westminster, and Dean of Theology at Corpus Christi College in London, speaks of the history of papal infallibility:

"The first problem about infallibility is that the New Testament makes it plain that Peter himself made tremendous errors both before and after Jesus died.

"After Jesus' resurrection, Peter made a very serious blunder. 'Heresy' is not too bad a word for it. The Church's greatest canon lawyer, Gratian, said in 1150: *'Petrus cogebat Gentes Judaizare et a veritate evangelii recedere'*: 'Peter compelled the Gentiles to live as Jews and to depart from Gospel truth.'"

Agreeing, then, with the only valid interpretation of the famous "Petrine Passage" (Matthew 16:18), Dr. De Rosa adds his voice to the almost unanimous conclusion of modern historical research and the authentic witness of the early Christian Church:

"There is, however, another interpretation of this text with a better pedigree than most Catholics realize. It may jolt them to hear that the great Fathers of the Church saw no connection between it and the pope. Not one of them applies 'Thou art Peter' to anyone but Peter. One after another they analyze it… Not one of them calls the Bishop of Rome a Rock or applies to him *specifically* the promise of the Keys. This is staggering to Catholics.

"The surprises do not stop there. For the Fathers, it is Peter's faith — or the Lord in whom Peter has faith — which is called the Rock, not Peter. All the Councils of the Church from Nicæa in the fourth century to Constance in the fifteenth agree that Christ himself is the only foundation of the Church, that is, the Rock on which the Church rests.

"There is no hint of an abiding Petrine *office*. In so far as the Fathers speak of an office, the reference is to the episcopate in general. All bishops are successors to all the apostles."

In the Middle Ages, the idea of a pope unable to fall into error took root within a hypothesis labelled "the work of Satan" by popes and curia alike. However, most Roman Catholics would be shocked at the pronouncement of the 16th century pope, Adrian VI, and the clear witness of history, which has been blurred out of focus by the Roman Church since 1870:

**"MANY ROMAN PONTIFFS WERE HERETICS."**

The quote is not in fact from a Protestant, but from Pope Adrian VI in 1523:

"If by the Roman Church you mean its head or pontiff, it is beyond question that he can err even in matters touching the faith. He does this when he teaches heresy by his own judgement or decretal. In truth, many Roman pontiffs were heretics."

The themes of papal heretics and popes excommunicated by the Church used to be common in theology, but little has been heard of them since 1870.

Other early examples, and the historical evidence, just will not go away; they return to haunt researchers:

"Pope Pelagius (556-60) talks of heretics separating themselves from the Apostolic *Sees*, that is, Rome, Jerusalem, Alexandria plus Constantinople. In all the early writings of the hierarchy, there is no special mention of a role for the Bishop of Rome, nor yet the special name of 'Pope'."

Many important and salient advances in historical research have taken place within the past twenty or thirty years. In light of this, Peter De Rosa mentions a few pertinent ideas connected with the total absence of early Church witness to this very recent doctrine of papal infallibility:

"Another astonishing omission in view of Vatican I: of the eighty or so heresies in the first six centuries, not one refers to the authority of the Bishop of Rome, not one is settled by the Bishop of Rome. Episcopacy in general sometimes comes under attack; no one attacks the authority of the Roman pontiff, *because no one has heard of it.*

"We already noted that not a single Father can find any hint of a Petrine office in the great Biblical texts that refer to Peter. Papal supremacy and infallibility, so central to the Catholic Church today, are simply not mentioned. Not a single creed, nor confession of faith, nor catechism, nor passage in patristic writings contains one syllable about the pope, still less about faith and doctrine being derived from him.

"The first pope to appeal to anything like what we know today as papal authority was Agatho in 680. He did so for a very embarrassing reason: a predecessor of his, Pope Honorius, was about to be condemned by a General Council for heresy.

"A day or two before the definition [of the Immaculate Conception] in 1854, the pope's private secretary, Monsignor Talbot, said in confidence to a friend: 'You see, the most important thing is not the new dogma but the way it is proclaimed.' Frankly, the pope was slipping in, so to speak, his own infallibility.

"The English-speaking world was far from unanimous in accepting papal infallibility. In 1822, Bishop Barnes, the English Vicar Apostolic, said:

'...in England and Ireland I do not believe *any* Catholic maintains the infallibility of the pope.' Later still, Cardinal Wiseman, who in 1850 headed the restored hierarchy of England and Wales, said: 'The Catholic Church holds a dogma often proclaimed that, in defining matters of faith, *she* (that is, the Church, not the pope) is infallible.' He went on: 'All agree that infallibility resides in the unanimous suffrage of the Church.'"

Lastly, it cannot be stressed enough that many of the ideas inherent in the recent innovations regarding papal infallibility had their roots and core in the numerous forgeries of the first millenium of Christianity. These forged documents were discredited several hundred years ago during the Reformation. De Rosa writes:

"Looking ahead for a moment, the documents forged in Rome at this time were systematized in the mid-1100's at Bologna by Gratian, a Benedictine monk. His *Decretum,* or Code of Canon Law, was easily the most influential book ever written by a Catholic. It was peppered with three centuries of forgeries and conclusions drawn from them, with his own fictional additions. If the 324 passages he quotes from popes of the first four centuries, only eleven are genuine.

"Looking further ahead to the thirteenth century, the *Decretum* was Thomas Aquinas' source-book for quotes from the Fathers and the popes when he came to write his masterly *Summa Theologica,* the second most renowned work by a Catholic. Aquinas, who knew little or no Greek, was led astray by Gratian, especially in regard to the papacy. Aquinas, of course, had immense influence on the Church, especially during the First Vatican Council when papal infallibility was defined.

"It was not until 1789 that Pius VI, in response to an enquiry from the German bishops, admitted that the Decretals were a forgery. The admission was nine centuries overdue. As [H. C.] Lea wrote in his *Studies in Church History* (1883):

'It is not the least of the troubles of an infallible Church that it cannot decently abandon any position once assumed. Having received the false decretals as genuine, and having based upon them its claims to universal temporal supremacy, when it was obliged to abandon the defence of the forgeries it was placed in a shockingly false position. To have endorsed a lie, from the ninth to the eighteenth century, was bad enough, but to give up the fruits of that lie, so industriously turned to profitable account, was more than could be reasonably expected of human nature."

# BIBLIOGRAPHY


Achtemeier, Paul J., ed: *Harper's Bible Dictionary;* Society of Biblical Literature, Harper and Row; New York;1985

Barclay, Wm.: *Gospel of Matthew; Daily Study Bible Series;* Westminster Press; Philadelphia, PA; 1957

Bettenson, Henry, ed.: *The Early Christian Fathers;* Oxford University Press; London, 1956.

Bettenson, Henry, ed.: *Documents of the Christian Church;* Oxford University Press; New York, 1963.

Bermejo, Luis M., S.J.: *Towards Christian Reunion;* University Press of America; Lanham, MD; 1984, 1987

Boettner, Loraine: *Roman Catholicism;* Presbyterian Reformed Publishing Co., Inc.; Phillipsburg, NJ; 1986 (25th printing)

Brown, Raymond E.; and Meier, John P.: *Priest and Bishop: Biblical Reflections,* Paulist Press; Paramus, NJ; 1970

Brown, Raymond J.: *Antioch and Rome;* Geoffrey Chapman; London; 1983

Butler, Dom Cuthbert: *Vatican I; Commentary Vol. I.;*Newman; Westminster, MD; 1962

Chadwick, Henry, and von Campenhausen, Hans: *Jerusalem and Rome,* Fortress Press; Philadelphia, PA; 1966

Chadwick, Henry: *The Early Church;* Penguin Books; Harmondsworth, Middlesex, England; 1977

Cullman, Oscar: *Peter: Disciple, Apostle, Martyr;* Westminster Press; Philadelphia, PA; 1958

Denzinger, H., and Schonmetzer, A., eds: *Enchiridion Symbolorum;* Barcelona, Rome, Freiburg: Herder; 1967; 1973 (36th ed.)

Eusebius: *Ecclesiastical History,* Penguin Press; Harmondsworth, Middlesex, England; 1984 ed.

Frend, W. H. C.: *The Rise of Christianity;* Fortress Press; Philadelphia, PA; 1984

Gentz, Wm. H., ed: *Dictionary of the Bible and Religion;* Abingdon; Nashville, TN; 1986

Granfield, Patrick: *The Limits of the Papacy;* Crossroads; New York; 1987

Guettée, Abbé: *The Papacy,* Minos Press; New York; 1866

Hasler, A. B.: *Papal Infallibility and the First Vatican Council;* Päbste und Rapsttum; Munich; 1970

Hasler, August B.: *How the Pope Became Infallible;* Doubleday; Garden City, NJ; 1981 (Extensive bibliography)

Hebblethwaite, Peter: "What if Vatican I Was Rigged"; article, *National Catholic Reporter;* Kansas City, MO; April 10, 1981

Herr, William: *This Our Church;* Thomas More Press; Chicago; 1986

Holy Bible, various translations (according to quotation used in text)

Huelin, Gordon, ed: *Old Catholics and Anglicans (1931-1981);* Oxford University Press; Oxford; 1983

*Infallible Fallacies;* Society for Promotion of Christian Knowledge; London; 1953

Jurgens, Wm., ed: *Faith of the Early Fathers;* Vols. I-III; Liturgical Press; Collegeville, MN; 1975

Juris, Paul: *The Rock* (tract); privately printed; Hopkins, MN; (ND)

Kelly, J. N. D.; *The Oxford Dictionary of the Popes;* Oxford University Press; Oxford, England; 1987

Kokkinakis, Bp. Athenagoras: *Christian Orthodoxy and Roman Catholicism;* Greek Orthodox Archdiocesan Press; New York; 1956 (booklet)

Kung, Hans: *Infallibility, an Inquiry;* Doubleday; Garden City, NJ; 1971

Livingstone, E.A.; *Oxford Dictionary of the Christian Church;* Oxford University Press; Oxford, England; 1977.

Mansi, J.D.: *Sacrorum conciliorum nova et amplissima collectio;* Welter Pub.; Leipzig; 1927

Mastrontonis, George, ed: *Epitome of Sacred Canons;* Logos Publishing; St. Louis, MO; 1962

McKenzie, John: *Dictionary of the Bible;* Bruce Publishing Co.; Milwaukee, WI; 1965

Meyendorff, J., et al.: *The Primacy of Peter;* Faith Press; Leighton, Bedfordshire, England; 1973

Meyendorff, John: article in *Orthodox Church* newspaper (April 1979); Syosset, LI, New York

Meyendorff, John: *Catholicity and the Church;* St. Vladimir's Press; Crestwood, NY; 1983

Moss, C.B.: *The Old Catholic Movement,* SPCK; London; 1964; Includes complete "Syllabus of Errors"

O'Connor, D.W.: *Peter in Rome;* Columbia University Press; New York; 1969

Patrinacos, Nicon: *Dictionary of Greek Orthodoxy;* Hellenic Heritage Pub.; Pleasantville, NY; 1984

Piepkorn, Arthur: *Profiles in Belief;* Vol. I; Harper and Row; New York; 1977

Roberts, A., and Donaldson, J., eds: *Ante-Nicene Fathers: Writings of the Early Church Fathers;* Vol. V; Eeerdmans; Grand Rapids, MI; 1980

Rockwood, Perry: *Babylon the Great and the Antichrist* (booklet); Halifax, NS, Canada; (ND)

Simons, Bishop F.: *Infallibility, the Evidence;* Templegate; Springfield, IL; 1968

Strossmayer, Bishop: *Bishop Strossmayer's Speech to Vatican Council I;* Florence, Italy; 1872 (translation)

Tierney, Brian: *Origins of Papal Infallibility (1150-1350): A Study of the Concepts of Infallibility;* "Studies in the History of Christian Thought," Vol. VI; Leiden; 1972

*Time* magazine: "Was Vatican I Rigged?" (article); Nov. 14, 1977; p. 52

Tuchman, Barbara: *A Distant Mirror;* Alfred Knopf, Inc.; New York; 1978

von Campenhausen, Hans: *Tradition and Life in the Church: Essays and Lectures on Church History;* Collins Press; St. James Place; London; 1968

von Campenhausen, Hans: *Ecclesiastical Authority and Spiritual Power in the Church of the First Three Centuries;* Stanford University Press; Standford, CA; 1969.

von Döllinger, Ignatz: *The Papacy and the Council,* Munich; 1869

von Hügel, Friedrich: *Notes on the Petrine Claims,* Sheed and Ward; London; 1930

Ward, C.M.: "Does the Church Need a Pope?"; article, *The Evangelist;* Port Allen, LA; May 1986

Young, Fr. Alexey: *Christianity or the Papacy?* (booklet); Nikodemos Orthodox Publishing Society; Etna, CA; (ND). Reprints available from The St. John of Kronstadt Press, Liberty, TN 37095